THE INTERPRETATION OF MUSIC

D1043124

MUSIC

_____

Editor

SIR JACK WESTRUP

M.A., B.MUS., F.R.C.O., HON. D.MUS.

*Heather Professor of Music in the
University of Oxford*

THE INTERPRETATION
OF MUSIC

THURSTON DART M.A.

*Professor of Music in the University
of Cambridge*

HUTCHINSON UNIVERSITY LIBRARY
LONDON

HUTCHINSON & CO. (*Publishers*) LTD
178-202 Great Portland Street, London, W.1

London Melbourne Sydney
Auckland Bombay Toronto
Johannesburg New York

★

First published 1954
Second (revised) impression 1955
Third impression 1958
Fourth (revised) impression 1960
Fifth impression 1962
Sixth impression 1964

Set in eleven point Imprint
and printed in Great Britain by
Fisher, Knight & Co. Ltd., at the
Gainsborough Press, St. Albans, Herts

CONTENTS

Out of the true plain song they judged the melody;
Curious conveying hideth much harmony.
Therefore of the plain notes to set a sure ground
Maketh a modulation of most perfect sound.
In curiosity oftimes truth slippeth by
And in the plain true notes all the sweetness doth lie.

(*Leckingfield proverb*)

PREFACE

IN preparing this book I have been greatly encouraged by the sympathetic interest shown in its progress by many of my friends, particularly those who live in Cambridge. I am especially grateful to two of them, Mr C. L. Cudworth and Mr Nigel Fortune, for reading the whole book through in typescript or in galley-proof and for making many helpful comments and suggestions; most of these have been incorporated in the text as it now stands. Mr Cudworth was kind enough to draw my attention to several early sources that I might otherwise have missed; Mr Fortune was generous with his help in the preparation of the index.

But my greatest sense of indebtedness is towards someone who did not see the book until it was published: Professor Charles van den Borren, of Brussels. Constant in his friendship as in his advice and guidance, he has been to more than one young scholar a pattern of knowledge matched by musicianship, of kindliness blended with humility, that outstrips emulation just as it inspires devotion. Without him this book could not have been begun; it was completed on the day he entered his eightieth year, and it is offered to him as a tribute.

Jesus College,　　　　　　　　　　　　　　　THURSTON DART
Cambridge.
November 1953.

A

CHAPTER I

THE PROBLEM

THE arts of mankind may be grouped together in a number of different ways. For instance, a convenient division may be made between the visual arts—painting, sculpture, architecture, mime—the aural arts—music, spoken verse—and those which depend for their effect on a combination of the two—rhetoric, theatre, opera, ballet. Or again the arts may be divided into those which are created once for all—sculpture, architecture, cinema—and those which need re-creation on every occasion that they are to be experienced; thus each performance of a play or a dance or a piece of music is a unique phenomenon which may be similar to other performances of the same work but can never be said to be identical with them.

These re-creative arts, the temporal arts as they are usually called, have one thing in common. All of them depend in one way or another upon a set of visual symbols which convey the artist's intentions to the performer and, through him, to the listener or the spectator. For the present discussion, the wide field of symbols must be narrowed down to those used in western civilization for the arts of literature and music, though there are of course many other sets that are thereby excluded—rather arbitrarily, perhaps. The literary arts use a basic set of symbols, the Roman alphabet, which has taken some 3,000 years to develop and has ousted several elaborate systems on the way. The musical arts use an entirely different system, staff notation; and though its period of continuous development has been shorter—perhaps no more than 1,500 years—its task is very much greater.

The system in use for literature is one that presents certain analogies, some stimulating and others quite false, with that in use for music. To begin with, the alphabet is a system that serves two purposes. It can be understood visually, and it can also be turned into sound; but it is not necessary to hear a book in order to understand what it means. The musical system *must* be heard if it is to have significance, for though the written symbols can be understood visually, they are merely a highly stylized representation of the music and not the music itself. To think otherwise, to analyse the black dots as though they were music, to compose them into an intellectually or visually pleasing pattern without reference to their implied sounds: activities of this kind are not concerned with music but with its symbols, and in music the ear, not the eye, is the only judge. Secondly, the ways in which alphabetic symbols are grouped together to make words and language will vary from country to country and from period to period, so that the same group of symbols will usually have different sounds and different meanings in different countries, and both sound and meaning will change over the course of the centuries. Thus in France and in England the letter-group 'p a y s' will have two separate pronunciations and two separate meanings. Musical notation has no meaning, in the sense that a word has a meaning, though it has significance; but the significance of, for instance,

in eighteenth-century France was quite different

from its significance in eighteenth-century England. Thirdly, a single concept will be expressed in different languages by different arrangements of letter-symbols; thus 'Pferd', 'cheval', 'horse', 'cavallo' are exact equivalents in different languages of the single concept 'horse'. Similarly, at various places and during various periods of musical history, quite different methods have been used for writing down one and only one musical concept.

At this point the reader may well feel a little dizzy, beginning to wonder, perhaps, what all this talk of meaning and of symbols has to do with how to play Byrd, Bach or Beethoven, none of whom was foolish enough to waste time in rather bumbling philosophical speculation. Its justification must be this: the musical notation in use today is the logical development of that used in earlier times, but the present-day significance of the symbols may be, and very often is, utterly different from their significance in eighteenth-century France or sixteenth-century England or fourteenth-century Italy. Modern notation is far more precise in matters of tempo, dynamics, rhythm, instrumentation, pitch, the duration of notes and so on, than it has been in any earlier century (though this is not necessarily a sign of musical health; but that is too big a question to be dealt with here). A twentieth-century composer uses notation in accordance with the conventions of his own time, and there is therefore little chance that a twentieth-century performer will misunderstand him. A composer of the eighteenth or the sixteenth or the fourteenth century also used notation in accordance with the conventions of his own time, but there is therefore every chance in the world that a twentieth-century performer will entirely misinterpret his music through an inadequate knowledge of these conventions, for the most part long obsolete and forgotten. In a word, when a modern performer looks at a piece of early music he must not take for granted the significance of any of the symbols he sees.

An example or two may make this clearer. Today the symbol for a breve is exceedingly rarely used; when it does occur it is interpreted as a very long note indeed. To the men of the twelfth century a breve, as its name suggests, was brief; it was in fact the shortest note then in existence. Today a breve always contains four minims; in the fourteenth century it might contain anything from four to twenty-four, according to the nationality of the man who wrote it down on paper and the context in which it occurs. Today the time-signature 3/2 is a time-signature and no more; to the fifteenth century it denoted pace as well as the metrical structure of the music. Today a dot after a note lengthens it by one-half, but in the seventeenth and eighteenth centuries it often lengthened it by very much more. Today a vertical dash over a note means that it is to be played staccatissimo; in the eighteenth century the identical symbol was used to mean a simple staccato. Today a sarabande is usually considered a slow dance; in the first half of the seventeenth century it was a very fast one.

The interpretation of early music is therefore a most complicated matter and the primary evidence, musical notation, on which our interpretation must necessarily be based has to be examined with the greatest care. First of all we need to know the exact symbols the composer used; then we must find out what these signified at the time they were written; and lastly we must express our conclusions in terms of our own age, for we live in the twentieth century and not in the eighteenth or the fifteenth. It is not easy to say which of these tasks should be carried out by the editor and which by the performer; all of them are important and all of them require a high sense of responsibility and a good deal of knowledge and taste. Moreover the performer was in earlier times regarded as a more intelligent member of the musical community than he is now, if the markings of dynamics, phrasing, tempo and what-not scattered over a modern work are any indication of the composer's attitude towards the performer; the further we go back in musical history, the rarer such markings become and the more trust was evidently placed in a performer's training, his sense of tradition, and his innate musicianship.

In the chain between composer and audience, the editor is an earlier link than the performer and he must therefore be considered first. It is clear from the above discussion that he must go carefully; he must show which features of the text placed in front of the performer are the composer's direct orders and which are his own subordinate suggestions, added in accordance with his knowledge of the best and the worst practices of the time. If the editor neglects this essential part of his duties as a member of the musical hierarchy, then the performer cannot know which parts of the printed page provide the evidence he will need for his interpretation; the editor's work is no longer a mere coat of protective varnish through which the composer's picture shines undimmed, but a whole set of brush strokes using the same painting technique and materials as the original artist (or, what is even worse, entirely different ones). Is this slur, this tempo mark, this phrasing, this note, in the original text? Or is it just a whim of the editor's? Where did the editor find the music itself? When and where was it written and first performed? What instruments did the composer have in mind here? What kind of sound did he want there?

Every performer has the right to ask these questions, just as anyone who looks at a painting has the right to ask similar ones of its curator, and every editor's duty is to see that they can be answered as easily and as authoritatively as possible; he is the curator of the music and no more. 'As easily as possible': that will mean that the performer must be given a text he can understand, one that—as far as it can—uses the symbols of notation with the senses that he is accustomed to give them. This is the only way in which the performer's attitude of mind to the music can be made to resemble that of its original interpreter. For instance, we are brought up to think of semibreves as long notes; but to print a modern edition of fifteenth-century music in its original semibreve note-values is to suggest to the twentieth-century performer that it is slow music, whereas to the fifteenth-century composer and performer a semibreve meant much the same thing that a crotchet does today. It was the standard unit of time; nowadays the most commonly used unit of time is the crotchet, which may therefore suitably replace it. 'As authoritatively as possible': the only man who knows exactly how he wants his music to be performed is presumably the composer himself, whether he is a man of the fifteenth century or a man of our own time. Consequently every scrap of information that an early composer conveyed to his performer by means of the written notation he used must be treated as though it were gold; it is very precious, and far more valuable than any editor's opinion, however enlightened this may be. Moreover, though many features of early notation that once meant something are still only imperfectly understood today, despite the continuous and careful work of more than six generations of scholars, that is no reason for eliminating them altogether from a modern text; an editor who does so is a barbarian and a false custodian of the treasures of the past.

The editor, then, must provide a good text. The performer, like the editor, must find out all he can about how the music of an earlier age was performed by contemporary musicians; they knew far more about it than he does, and fortunately they did not rely entirely on oral tradition to pass on what they knew. An enormous amount of information about the performance of early music survives in contemporary sources, not only in treatises specifically dealing with the problem o interpretation, but also in prefaces, essays, marginal notes, pictures, sculptures, miniatures, and descriptions in verse or prose of concerts, feasts, church services and amateur music-making. Sometimes the information is tantalizingly insufficient; medieval music, for example, can never be brought to life with the same authenticity that should characterize performances of baroque music but in fact too seldom does. Sometimes the information is too copious, and the sources too conflicting and confusing, for the scholar to be able to handle it in a little space; thus to give an exact set of directions for the performance of all musical ornaments whatsoever would fill three books the size of the present one. Often the information comes from little men of immense pretensions, whose remarks have to be scrutinized with great care and weighed against less wordy but more accurate writers. Thus Kircher's *Musurgia* (1650) is often referred to by writers on seventeenth-century music as though it were written by Monteverdi, Purcell, and Lully rolled into one; but Kircher was merely a verbose and surprisingly credulous Jesuit priest with a taste for music and mechanics, and though his book is encyclopaedic in scope it is quite unreliable in detail.

Lastly, the information supplied by these sources must be strictly limited in its application. Certain modern students of interpretation have become so glutted by the rich feast of information at their disposal, good and bad, early and late, that they are quite capable of presenting the listener with a fifteenth-century song harmonized in the manner of the late sixteenth century, or with viol fantasies by Byrd and his English contemporaries played in a style that was fashionable for perhaps eight or ten years at the court of Frederick the Great.

The subject is vast, fascinating, and little understood, and its pitfalls are numerous, large and uncommonly deep. Boldness is better than timidity, perhaps, and this book will therefore set out to survey some of the problems involved in the present-day performance of music written between 1350 and 1850. The survey is bound to be little more than a sketch; it is not a map, but rather a chart in the style of those of the sixteenth century, embellished with unknown names and tracts of unexplored ground, and not drawn to scale. Some topics will be discussed in extravagant and almost unendurable detail, and many will be dismissed altogether. Some attempt will be made to suggest fruitful lines of approach to the music of those composers particularly esteemed at the present day, and whenever possible the original sources will be quoted and used as the basis of the discussion. Musical examples in the text must necessarily be few if the book is not to become unreasonably expensive, and in many places the reader will be referred to editions that are not as readily accessible as one might wish. Whenever possible, musical illustrations will be drawn from the two volumes of the *Historical Anthology of Music* (Oxford University Press). HAM 230, for instance, will denote no. 230 of this collection.

CHAPTER II

THE EDITOR'S TASK

THE musical score as we know it today was developed during the last two centuries or so. In most scores published today there are full indications of the instrumentation of the music, exact nuances of dynamics and tempo, ornaments, bowings, phrasings and all the rest of it. When the work in question is one that was written during the last hundred years or so, we can be fairly certain that most of the these markings are the authentic voice of the composer; but the older the music, the greater the likelihood that most if not all of them are no more than expressions of opinion on the part of the editor. In the whole of the first book of the '48', for instance, there are in the original manuscripts only four tempo marks (three of them in Prelude 2, one in Fugue 24); and slurs occur only in the subjects of Fugues 6 and 24, and—with a different meaning—in the last bar of Fugue 10. Anything else found in a modern edition of these works is certainly not by Bach. In the Fitzwilliam Virginal Book there are no phrasings and no tempo marks at all, and the same is true of most of the music of the Renaissance.

But it is regrettably difficult to find modern editions of old music in which any distinction is made between the composer's own markings and those that the editor, for one reason or another, has seen fit to add. As a result of this combination of editorial highhandedness and irresponsible publishing most twentieth-century music students are deceived into seeing early music through the eyes of someone quite other than the composer. They buy an edition of the '48' or of Haydn's keyboard sonatas and go to a great deal of trouble to follow the printed tempi, phrasing and dynamics, assuming in all innocence that these markings are those of Bach or Haydn when nine times out of ten they are merely those of Herr X or Dr Y, or even of Herr X, amended by Dr Y, and thoroughly revised by the eminent pianist, Mr Z. A lead in the right direction has been given by several German publishing houses with their *Urtext* ('original text') editions, in which the composer's own notes and markings are exactly shown and every editorial addition, interpolation or interpretation is clearly distinguishable, and the Associated Board of the Royal Schools of Music has been responsible for some notable editions of the same kind. Here is a select list of some *Urtext* editions of early keyboard music, for instance, in which the student can see the original texts for himself, and make up his own mind whether he wishes to adopt the editor's suggestions or not. Some of the editions are expensive or out-of-print or both; but they will be found in the leading libraries, so that a student may compare them with his own edition and satisfy himself of the answers to any queries he may have. The list cannot claim to be exhaustive, and no doubt there are many omissions; but it will do to begin with.

Arne	8 Sonatas	Augener, ed. Pauer
Bach	Goldberg Variations	Schirmer, ed. Kirkpatrick
	Organ works	Novello, ed. Emery
	Suite in C minor	Schott, ed. Ferguson
	Keyboard works	Peters, ed. Soldan
	Keyboard works	Henle, ed. Steglich
Bach, C. P. E.	Keyboard works	Breitkopf & Härtel, ed. Krebs
Beethoven	Keyboard works	Henle
Buxtehude	Keyboard works	Hansen, ed. Bangert
Couperin	Keyboard works	Lyre-Bird Press, ed. Brunold (part of complete works). Augener, ed. Brahms and Chrysander

Elizabethan and Jacobean Composers:

	Byrd: My Ladye Nevells Book	Curwen, ed. Andrews
	45 Pieces	Lyre-Bird Press, ed. Tuttle
	Parthenia	Stainer & Bell, ed. Dart
	Morley: Keyboard music	Stainer & Bell, ed. Dart
	Tisdall: Keyboard music	Stainer & Bell, ed. Ferguson

Elizabethan and Jacobean Composers:

	Bull: Keyboard music	Stainer & Bell, ed. Steele, Cameron and Dart
	The Mulliner Book	Stainer & Bell, ed. Stevens
	Tomkins: Keyboard music	Stainer & Bell, ed. Tuttle
Frescobaldi	Keyboard music	Bärenreiter, ed. Pidoux
A. Gabrieli	Keyboard works	Bärenreiter, ed. Pidoux
	Aylesford pieces	Schott, ed. Fuller Maitland
Haydn	Sonatas	Peters, ed. Martienssen
Merulo	Canzoni (1592)	Bärenreiter, ed. Pidoux
Mozart	Keyboard works	Henle, ed. Wallner
Purcell	Keyboard works	Stainer & Bell, ed. Dart
Rameau	Keyboard works	Bärenreiter, ed. Jacobi
Scarlatti	60 sonatas	G. Schirmer, ed. Kirkpatrick
Sweelinck	Keyboard works	Alsbach, ed. Seiffert (edn. of 1943)
Telemann	36 Fantasien	Bärenreiter, ed. Sonnenschein

To draw up a similar list for vocal, orchestral and chamber music would not be easy. But there are certain ways in which all these reliable editions can be recognized—finger-prints, as it were—and the wise student will look for them. Not every edition will use them all, of course; there is still no internationally accepted convention for the editing of old music, though great strides are now being made towards it, and many current editions are either too scholarly (and therefore unintelligible to the average musician) or else too slovenly (and therefore dangerous to the student and contemptible to the scholar). Yet there is no reason why an edition should not satisfy the needs of both the performer and the scholar. *Musica Britannica*[1] is an example; so are most of the editions listed above. Any editor who makes use of some or all of the follow-

[1] A national collection of music, published for The Royal Musical Association by Stainer & Bell.

ing suggestions will be working on the right lines; the performer who wants to make certain that he is getting material on which he can safely base his interpretation of early music will be well advised to see that at least some of these identifying marks are present in the edition he is going to buy. Many of the suggestions may perhaps be rather idealistic, but the majority of editors have only themselves to blame for the fact that the matter is discussed in such detail here.

HINTS TO EDITORS

(1) Make certain that your contribution to the edition can be distinguished from the composer's. Thus original expression marks should be in heavy type, your own in light type; the composer's music should be in full-sized music type, your additions in a smaller size. Or you may use other typographical dodges: square brackets, for instance, or slurs with a dash(⌒). The details of the convention you adopt are comparatively immaterial; but the convention itself must be there. The composer's accidentals should be in front of the notes to which they refer; any missing ones supplied by you should be in smaller type above (or in front of) the notes, and they should hold good to the end of the bar. Eliminate redundant accidentals, and use today's notational conventions wherever you can; a semi-facsimile of the original is of no use to the scholar and it is a nuisance to the performer. If it is more convenient and less fussy, editorial additions may be placed in square brackets. Similarly your written-out continuo part may look better in normal-sized notes, but in this case warn the player somewhere of what you have done.

(2) Provide the player and the scholar with some convenient reference marks. This elementary point is very often forgotten, and that means that hours of rehearsal and research time are wasted, and tempers become unnecessarily frayed. The best and most widely used convention is to number every fifth or tenth bar, printing these numbers in italics—which are conspicuous without being unsightly.

(3) Since the musical notation of our own time is more or less based on the crotchet as time-unit, make suitable adjust-

ments in earlier notation. This will usually mean a reduction
of note-values, sometimes by as much as eight or sixteen,
but there are occasions when the music will be made considerably more intelligible by an increase in its original note-
values. Thus certain passages in Beethoven's later piano
sonatas look immensely forbidding written in Beethoven's own
rather oddly chosen note-values (27/32 and so on), yet no
editor seems prepared to make them easier for the player by
writing them in longer notes. This point is an important one.
It has already been pointed out that to the fifteenth century
a semibreve was roughly the equivalent of what a crotchet is
to us. To publish old music as a string of breves, semibreves
and minims is wrong on two counts: first, because it gives the
performer a misleading idea of the proper tempo; and secondly,
because 'void' notes (the sixteenth-century term for notes like
these) are demonstrably less legible than 'full' ones (another
sixteenth-century term: crotchets and lower note-values). One
fault of the beautifully produced volumes of *Tudor Church
Music*, for instance, is that when seen from any distance the
notes softly and suddenly vanish away, like the Baker in 'The
Hunting of the Snark.'

(4) Use the most appropriate key-signature, i.e. the one
that will accord most closely with modern practice. Following
the convention of the time, Handel's so-called 'Harmonious
Blacksmith' variations were originally printed in a key-signature
of three sharps, even though they were unmistakeably in E
major, and every sharpened D was provided with a special
accidental of its own. Similarly many Dowland songs that are
in G major, to our way of thinking, were originally printed
with no key-signature at all—for all practical purposes, sharp
key-signatures were unknown until the early years of the
seventeenth century—and others in G minor appeared with a
key-signature of one flat, every E being individually flattened.
To reproduce obsolete conventions of this kind today is asking
for trouble, for they run counter to our musical training;
and if the change is properly made, the resulting text is not
one whit less scholarly than one which keeps more closely to
the original conventions. The same kind of change of key-
signature might well be made in certain passages to be found

in the keyboard and other music of the nineteenth century; Chopin, Schumann and Brahms are apt to modulate extremely while still retaining the original key-signature in which the movement began, and present-day publishers would often make the performer's task much easier by a little judicious alteration of the composer's notation.

(5) Use current clefs. This matter, like that of retaining original note-values, is another Pedant's Corner which needs a good sweeping out. Many 'scholarly' editions of old music are valueless to the average music-lover since they perpetuate the fallacy that choral singers of our own time sing from C-clefs. There were two reasons why C-clefs were so extensively used in early vocal music: for one thing, singers were taught to sing from them; for another—and this is one that is often overlooked —it was not easy to set up in type music that involved many ledger lines, and most printed music before 1700 or so (and much later music, for that matter) was set up from movable types. Consequently, the printer and the composer took some trouble to choose a clef which brought the part in question as nearly as possible within the compass of a five-line stave. Neither of these reasons holds good today. Singers sing from G-clefs and F-clefs; and music is usually printed by a lithographic process from engraved plates, which leave the engraver as much freedom as he likes. Soprano, mezzo-soprano and alto parts should be written in the normal treble clef, bass parts in the bass clef, and tenor parts in the so-called tenor clef (a treble-clef with a little 8 below it, to indicate that the notes sound an octave lower than they are written). This tenor clef is not the only one in use, but all the others are unsatisfactory in one way or another.

Three of the essential rules of any well-devised system of symbols, whether for music, for mathematics or for any other purpose are (i) that each symbol should have only one meaning; (ii) that any modification of a symbol should be extensible to all the other symbols in the set; (iii) that all the symbols of the same set should be readily distinguishable and of more or less the same size. To write a tenor part in the normal treble clef, with no indication of the implied transposition, breaks rule (i), and can lead to all kinds of trouble. To use a treble clef with a little c after it (as in *Tudor Church Music*), or combined with a C-clef (as in many Italian editions of old music), or immediately followed by another treble clef, will break either rule (ii) or rule (iii) or else both of them at once. None of these objections can be raised against the symbol suggested above, which is already in international use. And the use of a figure 8 to denote a transposition of an octave can be easily extended; a treble clef with an 8 above it is already in use for music for descant recorder, and a bass clef with an 8 below it has been found convenient for editions of early lute-music.

(6) Keep the scholar happy. He will want to know as far as possible what the original music looked like and, though nothing short of a collotype facsimile can hope to answer every question he may wish to ask, a properly planned modern edition can answer very many of them without unduly distracting the musician who merely wants to perform the music it contains.

(a) At the beginning of a polyphonic composition there should be a set of prefatory staves, one for each part, showing the original clef, the number of stave-lines (in certain instances this may provide vital information on how the music should be orchestrated, so that it must not be withheld), the original key-signature and time-signature, and the first sounding note. This takes up almost no room, yet it conveys a great deal of information; and the reader can see at once what the original notation was like.

(b) Two other features of early notation, ligatures and coloration, have passed entirely out of use for 300 years or so; yet both are important, to the performer as well as to the scholar, and both must therefore be indicated in a modern edition. A ligature was a compound symbol representing two or more successive notes: their pitch and duration were determined by the ligature's form, in accordance with certain sets of rules valid at various times and in various places. At first glance this may look like another piece of lumber stacked up in Pedant's Corner; but it seems that a ligature also denoted a legato manner of singing or playing, thus in a sense being equivalent to a modern slur. Moreover, in fifteenth-century music the number of ligatures found in a polyphonic part may often determine whether this part is instrumental or vocal, which is again a matter of great interest to the performer. Some sign must therefore be used to show which notes of a modern text were in ligature in the original. If the modern sign for a slur is used for this purpose, a single symbol will have been invested with two meanings, which is something to be avoided whenever possible; consequently it has become customary to use a squared-off version of a slur (⌐⌐) instead.

Coloration is too complicated a matter to be explained in detail here. Briefly, coloration was a special way of writing note-symbols which remained in use in one form or another up to the early years of the eighteenth century, and it affected the duration of the notes, their stressing, and in some cases, the speed of the whole piece. (Modern notation still contains one survival of coloration, for historically speaking a crotchet is a 'coloured' version of a minim.) Once again, coloration is a matter that is of some importance both to the scholar and to the performer, and in any worthwhile edition of old music the places where it occurs must be indicated. The accepted symbols, inconspicuous yet eloquent, are two small inverted Ls (⌐   ⌐), placed at the beginning and end of the passage concerned.

(c) Many of the writers of early vocal manuscripts seem to have treated the verbal texts in a very cavalier fashion. Sometimes these were omitted altogether, or else indicated only by the first few words; sometimes, as in many settings of the Mass, it is clear that the given words must be repeated and rearranged to fit the music; and often, as in many madrigals of the late sixteenth century, a number of conventional signs are used to denote repetitions of one kind or another. The exact way in which the words should be underlaid to the music is consequently a matter of considerable dispute among musical scholars, and it will be a long time before enough evidence has been assembled to enable them to act with complete confidence. Meanwhile, the music is waiting to be sung and enjoyed. The safe way out for the scholar would be to reproduce the original underlay exactly, but there is no satisfactory way of doing this, short of a photographic facsimile; and neither a facsimile nor a semi-facsimile will give the performer what he needs, a text ready for singing. The editor therefore has often to take the heavy responsibility of arranging the text in accordance with his best knowledge of how it was done in earlier times, and this is no easy matter since the traditional rules that must have been used in the fifteenth and sixteenth centuries were seldom set down in writing. In his theoretical treatise published in 1552, Adrian Petit Coclico, one of Josquin's pupils, stated that the first thing Josquin taught him, once he had acquired a mastery of the rudiments of music, was how to fit words and music together. But, tiresomely enough, neither Coclico nor any other writer of the Middle Ages and Renaissance saw fit to leave us a full description of how this was done. Scholars are slowly assembling a body of facts bearing on the question, but when it comes to preparing an edition much of the underlay must remain pure guesswork, and it is only fair to warn the buyer. The conscientious scholar, using a well-established convention, shows such underlay in italic type. This will not disturb the performer, and the scholar will be able to draw his own conclusions and to check his own research into the matter.

(7) Locate and identify the sources you have used. The interested music-lover and the scholar can then look at the originals for themselves. The identification should be full and precise; remarks like 'from a manuscript in the British Museum' or 'from the Original Edition' are useless.

(8) Warn the reader of any substantial changes made in the original text, but do it fairly inconspicuously. Changes should be few; when in doubt, leave them out. Dr Johnson's advice has lost none of its force in the 200 years since it was written:

> Some changes may well be admitted in a text . . . so long exposed to caprice and ignorance. But nothing shall be imposed . . . without notice of the alteration; nor shall conjecture be wantonly or unnecessarily indulged. It has long been found that

very specious emendations do not equally strike all minds with conviction; . . . and therefore, though perhaps many alterations may be proposed as eligible, very few will be obtruded as certain. . . . There is danger lest peculiarities should be mistaken for corruptions, and passages rejected as unintelligible, which a narrow mind happens not to understand.

(Preface to his edition of Shakespeare)

At the same time, certain characteristic features of early sources will need to be changed, or to be supplemented. Thus much fifteenth- and sixteenth-century music will require additional accidentals if it is to conform with the acknowledged customs of the time. These customs are not easily discovered, and many twentieth-century editors have repaid the liberality with which their nineteenth-century forbears strewed accidentals over the texts by a most miserly and grudging handful, or even by none at all. This is the Tale of the Emperor's New Clothes with a vengeance. . . . Some editorial accidentals will often be needed, and if these are printed fairly small, then those who do not like them can easily miss them out.

If it is the editor's considered opinion that certain notes in the original source are definitely wrong, then these should be altered in his printed text, the original reading being relegated to a footnote. This is a perfectly scholarly thing to do, and any other procedure is apt to lead to all kinds of difficulties and misunderstandings in rehearsal and performance.

(9) Distinguish between the words 'transcribe', 'edit', 'arrange', 'orchestrate', 'realize'. A transcription should be a literal reproduction of the original source; an edition should be a transcription ready for performance. An arrangement implies some alteration of the original—violins replacing viols, for instance, or voices interchanged. An orchestration will be a setting for some new and larger medium of a work originally written for more intimate performance. 'Realization' should properly be used only for written-out continuo parts. These distinctions are worthwhile, but they are too rarely observed.

(10) Provide the performer with a line or two about the music he is going to buy and play. You probably know more

than he will about its importance, its style and its history, and it is a pity to keep this information to yourself (if you do not know more, then you have no business to be editing the work). But make your preface short and readable; you are neither delivering a lecture nor applying for the Degree of Doctor of Philosophy.

CHAPTER III

SONORITIES

ONCE a satisfactory text has been provided, the next questions
the student of early music will ask are likely to be concerned
with the tone-colours appropriate to the particular piece or the
particular period he is studying. To decide what these were,
and to what extent they should or can be reproduced today is
one of the greatest problems of interpretation. A composer of
the past conceived his works in terms of the musical sounds of
his own day, just as a twentieth-century composer does, and
if we are to do justice to old music we must do our best to
discover what these sonorities were. Until recently this problem
was regarded in the light of what is usually called the evolutionary theory of music, which provided a comfortable solution
to this problem as to so many others. According to this theory,
the development of music had followed a fairly steady progress
towards its present perfection; eighteenth-century music,
musical instruments and methods of performance were better
than those of the seventeenth century, and nineteenth-century
music had made similar advances over the music of the eighteenth century. In the course of history the harpsichord had
been replaced by the piano, the recorder by the flute, the viols
by the violins, and if anyone wished to know the reason for
the changes the evolutionary theory gave a ready answer: the
poorer instrument had yielded its place to a better one. Consequently few musicians had any qualms about performing
harpsichord music on the piano or recorder music on the flute,
and it was rather automatically assumed that Bach and Handel
would have written their music for the modern grand piano
or the modern concert flute, if they had had the chance.

Pushed to its logical limits, this point of view leads to great
absurdities. If we assume that Bach and Handel would have
preferred to write for instruments that only acquired their
characteristically modern tone-qualities some hundred years

or more after both composers were in their graves, then we may argue similarly that Byrd would presumably have preferred to write for the early eighteenth-century harpsichord, and that the anonymous keyboard composers of the early fourteenth century would have considered their music to be heard at its best on an instrument of the kind described by Arnault of Zwolle, physician to the Duke of Burgundy, in the 1460s. All of which is ridiculous enough: but the alternative, according to the evolutionists, is to assume that all early composers whatsoever would have preferred to use the instruments of our own time, a point of view that makes us appear impossibly conceited and arrogant.

The first signs of a changing attitude towards these problems can be seen in the historical concerts that the great Belgian scholar Fétis gave in Paris more than a century ago. Fétis, whose musicology was an unstable mixture of science and instinct, went to considerable trouble to find instruments contemporary with the music he chose for his programmes, and—perhaps even more difficult—he persuaded various fine instrumentalists to spend a good deal of time learning how to find their way about on them. But his example was an isolated one; his ideas did not take hold, largely because old music was still regarded by him and his audience as something for the antiquary, the student and, to a quite considerable extent, the musical snob.

By the closing decades of the nineteenth century things had already begun to change. For one thing, the average concert programme was tending to include an ever-increasing proportion of old music—Beethoven, Haydn, Handel and, occasionally, even Bach. For another, a number of hard-working musical scholars had made fine editions of the music of a very large and representative selection of old composers. Their music was no longer accessible only to the trained scholar, the antiquary and the collector; anyone who had the money and the inclination could go and buy the complete works of Bach or Handel or Palestrina. This situation was very different from that existing a hundred years earlier. No one in 1790 could have bought the complete works of, say, Purcell or Palestrina even if he had wanted to; the few attempts that had been made at producing editions of early music were chiefly confined to England, where they were sponsored by a group of intelligent and fairly well-to-do amateurs, and regarded as a gentlemanly diversion and little more.

Some account of the quickening of interest in the performance of early music in this country may be found in George Bernard Shaw's shrewd and entertaining musical criticisms, written when he was a young man. He writes with great sympathy of the concerts given by Arnold Dolmetsch and his friends and relations in his house at Greenwich; he tells with wry amusement of how he once heard at a concert of old music what he took to be the jangling of a bell-wire—but it turned out to be only Dr Parry at a harpsichord. From the modest beginnings that he described an important movement slowly took shape and slowly gathered momentum. Obsolete instruments were lovingly restored, and eventually copies of them were made and their development taken up again at the point where it had ceased a century or so before. Players learned, after much hard work, how to handle these instruments—a very difficult task indeed, for though you can learn how to make a harpsichord by taking an old one to pieces, you cannot do the same thing with harpsichord-playing. In all these activities the fiery and impatient genius of Arnold Dolmetsch played a great part, though he was not the only worker in the field.

OBSOLETE INSTRUMENTS

The first instruments to be revived were the harpsichord and the clavichord. Indeed in England these instruments had remained alive, in a ghostly and tenuous fashion, since the eighteenth century; so had the tradition of playing from a figured bass, which many nineteenth-century organists learned from their predecessors and passed on to their pupils. Makers like Dolmetsch, Gaveau, Pleyel, Goble and Goff, players like Mrs Gordon Woodhouse, Wanda Landowska and Ralph Kirkpatrick, rival and perhaps even surpass the makers and players of earlier times; composers like Manuel de Falla, Francis Poulenc, Walter Leigh, Herbert Howells and Frank

Martin have found the unfamiliar tone-colours of the harp-sichord and clavichord stimulating and rewarding. And the enlightened policies of certain gramophone companies and, latterly, of the BBC have familiarized modern audiences with their sounds. It is no longer true, in fact, to call the harpsichord an obsolete instrument, though it is not always heard to its best advantage. To take only a single example: in works such as Bach's harpsichord concertos, accompanied by a modern string orchestra of fifteen or twenty players, the balance of loudness between orchestra and solo instrument will be com-pletely unlike what Bach's audience heard unless the harp-sichord's sound is amplified; if this is done by changes in its construction its true tone-colour and touch will suffer, yet if it is done by electrical means the purist will be outraged, the critics taken aback, and the orchestral players affronted.

Other instruments, too, are acquiring a new lease of life. The recorder, which is cheap, portable, easy to learn in the initial stages, and rich in repertory, is fast regaining some of its seventeenth- and eighteenth-century popularity as an amateur instrument. One or two groups of players and some individuals have reached very high standards of ensemble and technique, and a sign of the times is that in London it is now regarded as distinctly improper to perform works like Monteverdi's *Vespers* or Purcell's *Odes on St. Cecilia's Day* without recorders. The viols and the lutes are making slower progress. At least one viol consort (that of the 'Schola Cantorum Basiliensis') has achieved the finished ensemble and perfection of phrasing and intonation that one is used to expecting from a professional string quartet, and there are perhaps two or three skilled lutenists. But far too often extraordinary hybrid instruments appear on the concert platform that bear little or no resemblance to their ancestors; instruments such as those which have, rather happily, been christened 'cellambas'—viols heavily strung, played without frets and bowed overhand—'lutars'—lutes strung singly (like the guitar), with metal frets and wrongly shaped backs—and 'pianichords'—doctored pianos and castrated harpsichords. These instruments are not viols or lutes or harpsichords, but new instruments altogether. They may be good or bad—the future will decide that—but to fob them off on the listener as though they were authentic is to debauch his ear and to insult his intelligence; and it is doubtful whether the cause of old music is furthered by their well-meaning players, or by the happy pianists who sit at a proper harpsichord and play it like a grand piano, using the wrong touch, the wrong tempo, and no taste at all.

Impressive though the list of revived instruments undoubtedly is, there is much waiting to be done. Many early seventeenth-century instruments are still lost in limbo, and some of them will prove rewarding to those who are bold enough to bring them back to life. The pleasant snarl of the regal, rightly regarded in its own day as the perfect foil to the tone of trombones; the agile cornett, with a sound midway between that of a trumpet and a flute, which was once considered to be the closest instrumental equivalent to the human voice; the veiled and nutty reediness of the crumhorn; the nobility of the high harmonics of the natural trumpet; the soft supporting harmonies of a chamber organ; the romantic sound of the *chitarrone*, the perfect accompaniment to the vocal music of Caccini and Monteverdi: these and many other tone-colours cannot be forgotten by those who have been privileged to hear them played, even imperfectly and with inadequate preparation on the part of the player. And until they are once more made available—modern copies in the hands of proficient musicians —music is the poorer for their loss, and our ideas of the music of men like Monteverdi, Gabrieli and Schütz must remain quite imperfect.

ORCHESTRAL INSTRUMENTS

But the greatest obstacle to a true understanding of the music of Monteverdi, Gabrieli and Schütz, even of Mozart and Beethoven perhaps, does not lie in the difficulty of finding regals and regal-players, harpsichords and harpsichordists, or cornetts and cornettists. Few concert-goers probably realize that of all the instruments they hear in Beethoven's ninth symphony, for instance, the only ones whose sounds have not changed since the symphony was first performed in 1824 are the kettle-drum, the triangle, and the trombone. All the others have been

B

transformed, some more and some less, and even if the symphony is played with the same number of instruments and
voices that were used in 1824, the resultant sound will be quite
different in quality.

String-tone, for instance, has changed very much indeed,
the factors chiefly responsible for the change being the use
of wire strings for the topmost strings of a violin or a 'cello;
the violin chin-rest and the 'cello spike; the modern large-
sized viola; and the modern technique of the double-bass.
The true gut-string tone of a violin is now as obsolete as the
tone of a crumhorn or a regal. The almost universal custom of
using a chin-rest for the violin and a spike for the 'cello makes
it possible for a player to produce, without tiring, a vibrato
that is wider, quicker and used with far less discrimination
than it was 150 years ago. The Joachim quartet is believed to
be the first quartet that used the modern wide and almost
unremitting vibrato in their playing, and by no means all the
critics who heard them approved of the innovation. Paganini's
own manuscript markings in a copy of the *Caprices* direct the
pupil to use vibrato only at specific points, and not elsewhere.
What has been said here about vibrato must not be interpreted
to mean that all vibrato in old music is wrong, however.
Geminiani, for instance, in his treatise on musical taste (*c.* 1745)
says that 'the *Close Shake* [i.e. vibrato] . . . may be made on
any Note whatsoever'. Rousseau's tutor for the viol (1687)
recommends that it be used discreetly; so does Mersenne,
writing some fifty years earlier, and so does Ganassi, writing
a hundred years earlier still.

The large, and large-toned, viola is an admirable instrument for concertos and sonatas; but it is very much open to
question whether instruments of this kind have a proper place
in classical and romantic chamber music, for they profoundly
modify the balance of tone between the instruments of the
violin family that the composers had in mind. The technique
of the double-bass was transformed by virtuosi like Bottesini
and Dragonetti, and the modern orchestral double-bass player
achieves a far richer sonority from his overhand bowing and a
far more sensitive intonation from his more delicate left-hand
technique than did his nineteenth-century predecessors.

But until 1750 or so, the double-bass was only one of a pair of stringed instruments of the same tessitura, the other being the obsolete violone, or double-bass viol, with six fairly thin strings, frets, and a considerably smaller body than the double-bass proper. The clear resonance of the violone can etch a bass-line with great precision, and many composers from Monteverdi to Bach chose it instead of the double-bass.

WOODWIND AND BRASS

Woodwind tone has changed a good deal in the last century and a half, more particularly since 1900, and it varies very much from country to country. A modern concert flute or oboe is much more reliable and capable of playing considerably louder than its eighteenth-century ancestor, and the Boehm key-system has made it fully chromatic. But the tone has lost something in the process; the body of the instrument is loaded with a much greater weight of mechanism, which modifies and inhibits the natural resonance of the wood, and both instruments had a calmer and more pastoral tone in the eighteenth century. This may be judged not only from surviving examples when they are properly played, but also from the evidence of contemporary writers. The earliest extant tutor for the oboe was published in London in 1695, and its author—who was almost certainly the younger John Bannister—was at pains to point out in his preface the virtues of this new instrument: 'besides its Inimitable charming Sweetness of Sound (when well play'd upon) it is also Majestical and Stately, and not much Inferiour to the TRUMPET . . . [yet] all that play upon this instrument, to a reasonable perfection, know, That with a good Reed it goes as easie and as soft as the [recorder]'. Both flute and oboe were played in a less aggressively solo fashion in an eighteenth-century orchestra than they tend to be today; what is so often a relatively minor part in the score of the whole work was played less obtrusively, and vibrato was far rarer. Geminiani (c. 1745) directed that vibrato in the flute 'must only be made on long Notes', and he was writing of solo, not of orchestral, music.

The eighteenth-century bassoon, like the flute and the oboe
of the same period, was more capricious and temperamental
than its modern equivalent. But it was also far more sprightly
and plump, and the contrast between its different registers
was greater than it is on the sophisticated, bland Heckel
bassoons used in most orchestras today. The modern clarinet
is less woody and chuckling than its ancestor. The French
horn has now become a German horn; the wider bore and
rotary valves which became popular during the nineteenth
century resulted in more reliability and greater ease of playing,
particularly in the virtuoso passages written by many orchestral
composers of the last eighty years or so. Hand-stopping was
introduced in the 1750s, considerably changing the tone, and
the modern cupped mouthpiece, with its choked throat, has
changed the tone still more. Consequently the instrument has
lost much of the romantic and cheerful quality which was
regarded by the eighteenth century as its special glory. Avison
(1752) said 'the *Trumpet* and *French-Horn* . . . have pieces
of very different Styles adapted to them. The one, perhaps to
animate and inspire Courage; the other to enliven and chear
the Spirits. . . .' Playing a narrow-bore horn without hand-
stopping or valves was a precarious business, but the result
was well worth the extra effort involved. Anyone who has once
heard Brahms's horn trio played on a natural hand-stopped
valveless horn—the instrument for which it was written—
may well find other performances lacking in magic.

Valved trumpets are more reliable and more agile than the
eighteenth-century natural trumpets, but they have lost some
nobility. The so-called Bach trumpet of the present day is
only half the length of an eighteenth-century instrument, and
its tone can never have the ringing quality of its ancestor. But
to obtain these very high harmonics (the *clarino* register) from
a natural trumpet makes such merciless demands on a player's
lips and lungs that the special technique required has long
fallen into disuse, and there seems little chance of its ever
being revived. The sound of the trombone has altered less
than trumpet tone during the last 300 years, though the tenor
trombone made by Georg Neuschel of Nuremberg in 1557
(once owned by Canon Galpin and now the emblem of the

Galpin Society[1]) has a much sweeter and softer tone than its modern descendant. The Neuschel trombone can consort on equal terms with viols and recorders; with its thinner walls and less delicately shaped mouthpiece, the modern instrument cannot.

THE PIANO

The technical improvements in piano-construction made during the last century and a half have been very considerable. They include the introduction of a heavy cast-iron frame, heavier stringing, instantaneous damping, and the Schwander repetition action; as a result of these changes in its construction the tone of the instrument has been profoundly modified and, some might say, coarsened. The Viennese fortepianos of the Mozart period cannot rival the modern grand in loudness or in speed of repetition, but good surviving specimens suggest that our conception of Mozart's piano music is falsified by our unfamiliarity with the piano of his time. Mozart himself once said he preferred the pianos made by Stein of Augsburg, and one or two instruments by this maker and his contemporaries are still in existence. Properly restored, these instruments display the following characteristics. (1) A thinner soundboard, much less heavily loaded than a modern soundboard. (2) Lighter stringing, the bass strings being of brass. (3) Very light hammers with sharply tapering shafts. (4) Lighter dampers; on the fortepiano by Americus Backer (1775) in the Benton Fletcher collection, the dampers are so light that the vibrating string joggles them up and down. The resulting tone is brighter, thinner, more delicate and more resonant than it is on a modern piano. The gradation of tone from treble to bass is different, partly because the places at which the hammers strike the strings do not correspond to those used by modern piano-makers; the treble is weaker and more percussive, while the bass is more distinct and less blurred in chords. Some gramophone records of these early fortepianos have been issued by the more enterprising companies; they will be more illuminating than a

[1] A society for the investigation of the history and use of musical instruments, founded in 1946.

dozen paragraphs of description, and the reader is strongly recommended to hear them. (5) The simple so-called Viennese action was extremely easy to regulate and repair (not that there was in any case much to go wrong with it), and it demanded far less finger energy from the player in passage-work than does a modern escapement action. Extremely rapid repetitions and extreme loudness of tone were not possible; but since ornaments and trills played on a Viennese action demanded a slightly different finger technique from that required in normal passage-work, they thereby acquired a distinctive quality which set them in relief against their surroundings. (6) True *una corda* action: the 'soft' pedal slid the hammers gently to the left so that the player could reduce the number of sounding strings in the treble from three to two to one at will. (7) The dampers were often raised by a hand-stop instead of by the modern sustaining pedal. Moreover, on many instruments the dampers for the top part of the instrument were controlled by one hand-stop and the dampers for the bottom half of the instrument by another. This was the kind of mechanism Beethoven was writing for in the 'Moonlight' sonata, and it is quite impossible on any modern piano to reproduce the exact effect he had in mind. Beethoven noted pedal effects of all kinds with great precision but, once again, it is not easy to find a modern edition in which these are faithfully reproduced. Liszt's edition of 1857 remains one of the most reliable that has ever been printed.

The grand pianos of Beethoven's own time were more robustly built than those of the Mozart period, and pianos of the 1830s bear strong resemblances to those of the present day. But this does not mean that in using a modern grand piano for Chopin's music we are necessarily doing justice to his thought. His own preference was for a medium-sized piano, and his system of fingering and touch derived from the eighteenth-century tradition, based on the differing strengths and capabilities of the individual fingers. When he played he kept his elbows close to his sides, and no arm weight was ever used ('Only Germans play with great strength', he once remarked); his hands were in a simple natural position well to the front of the keys. He always chose the easiest fingering, changing fingers on a key as often as an organist; the style was always cantabile, based on legato finger-work, and not on the use of the sustaining pedal; and he used the true rubato (heard today only in the singing of such artists as Hoagy Carmichael and Dinah Shore) in which the rhythm of the tune sways about the fixed and unchanging metre of its accompaniment.

Any clavichordist can confirm that the whole of Chopin's system is a direct descendant of the eighteenth-century school of clavichord-playing represented at its best by C. P. E. Bach, and described in great detail in Part I of his monumental *Essay on the True Art of Playing Keyboard Instruments*, first published in 1753. C. P. E. Bach's direct pupils included J. C. Bach and Dussek, but his importance as a teacher depended far more on the influence of his music and of his book than on the reputations of his personal pupils. Haydn, who called the book 'the school of all schools'; Mozart, who wrote of C. P. E. Bach that 'he is the father, we are the children; those of us who do anything correctly learned it from him, and anyone who does not admit this is a scoundrel'; Beethoven, Clementi, Hummel (Holmes, writing in 1828, described Hummel's gliding, smooth, expressive style, his beauty of touch and the 'soul of his appoggiatura'); Cramer, Field, and Chopin—all based their technique and teaching methods on the system established by Carl Philipp Emanuel and derived, at least in part, from the playing of his father. But this tradition of key-board-playing has not continued unbroken to the present day; we should hear better piano-playing if it had. Czerny, originally taught by Beethoven from C. P. E. Bach's book, abandoned this distinctively eighteenth-century system of touch and fingering in favour of a system based on the equalization of all the fingers. His innumerable studies and instruction books were designed to develop this new touch in the pupil, and these works, together with his high reputation as a teacher, had succeeded in obliterating nearly all traces of the earlier style by the sixties or seventies of the last century. Certain modern teachers, notably Tobias Matthay, have developed systems which return to some of the basic principles embodied in C. P. E. Bach's *Essay*, but their ideas are very far from univers-ally accepted. Meanwhile it is unfortunately true to say that perhaps eight out of every ten concert performances of the keyboard music of Bach, Haydn, Mozart, Beethoven and Chopin take not the least account of the personal views these men are known to have expressed about the proper way in which their music should be played.

THE ORGAN

During the last 400 years the sound of the organ has been more completely transformed than the sound of any other musical instrument whatsoever. The traditional tracker action, associated with the instrument from the earliest times and giving the player the most intimate possible link between finger and pipe, has been ruthlessly swept aside in favour of electric or pneumatic systems necessitated by the great increase in size of the modern organ and the immoderately high wind pressures made possible by mechanical systems of blowing; but the delicacy of phrasing and articulation that characterized all good playing on a tracker-action organ has been swept aside too, and few organists of our own time realize that their interpretations of music written before 1800 are for the most part caricatures of the originals. Some enlightened players are giving a lead, but it will be a long time before their style is regarded by the generality of players as anything but quaint and irrational.

THE RENAISSANCE ORGAN

Very little can be said about medieval organs since none has survived intact to our own day. For the sixteenth century, however, there is a great deal of evidence and, broadly speaking, it is true to say that sixteenth-century organ-building followed two main lines of development seen at their clearest in the Italian and German organs of this period. Here are the specifications of two medium-sized organs built at about the same time for two churches of comparable importance, one in North Italy and the other in South Germany; and, for comparison, two other specifications of about the same period are given, one from France and one from Holland.

UDINE CATHEDRAL (1517)
one manual:

Tenori	8'	XXII	1'
Octave	4'	XXVI	$\frac{2}{3}'$
XV	2'	XXIX	$\frac{1}{2}'$
XIX	$1\frac{1}{3}'$	Flauti	(?4')

CONSTANZ CATHEDRAL (1516–20)
Great:

Prinzipal	8'	Zimbel III (very high	
Schwiegel	8'	ranks)	
Oktave	4'	Gedackt	8'
Quint	$2\frac{2}{3}'$	Gedackt	4'
Superoktave	2'	Posaune	8'
Hintersatz (large mixture)		Nonenpfeife	4'

Choir (behind the player):

Prinzipal	4'	Rohrflöte	4'
Oktave	2'	Quint	$1\frac{1}{3}'$
Spitzflöte	2'	Oktave	1'
Gedackt	8'	Zimbel (?III) very high ranks	
Hintersätzlein (small		Posaune	8'
mixture)		Regal	4'

Pedal:

Prinzipal	16'	Heerpauken (2 large pipes,
Oktave	8'	almost in unison, produc-
Oktave	4'	ing strongly marked beats
Quinte	$5\frac{1}{3}'$	and intended to sound like
Krummhorn	16'	a kettledrum)-
Posaune	8'	Vogelsang
Hintersatz (large mixture)		Zimbelstern

BORDEAUX, ST. MICHEL (begun 1510)
(probably) one manual:

Principal	8'	Cymballes III(?) ranks,	
Fourniture 8'+4'+2'		lacking tierce	
Papegay	$2\frac{2}{3}'$	Fleutes d'Almans	4'
Fleutes	8'	Regal	8'
Cornet 8'+4'+2$\frac{2}{3}$'+1'		(Nazard)	$1\frac{1}{3}'$

B*

OOSTHUIZEN, NORTH HOLLAND (1521)

one manual, pull-down pedals:

Bourdon 16' (originally 8'; probably a flute)		Quint	2⅔'
		Woudfluit	2'
Praestant 8'		Mixtuur II–III ranks	
Octaaf 4' (doubled pipes above *a'*)		Sesquiltera II ranks	
		Tremulant	

This picture of European organ-building during the sixteenth century may be usefully supplemented from Spain.

TOLEDO CATHEDRAL (1549)

Great:

(all stops divided into trebles and basses, separately controlled)

Flautado	16'	Trompeta real	8'
Violon	16'	Clarin de campana	4'
Flautado	8'	Clarin de claro	4'
Octava	4'	Clarin brillante	2'
		Trompeta magna (trebles only)	16'

Choir:

(all stops divided into trebles and basses, separately controlled)

Flautado	16'	Trompeta magna (trebles only)	16'
Flautado	8'		
Violon	8'	Trompeta real	8'
Octava	4'	Bajoncillo y clarin	8'+4'
Octava tapada	4'	Violetas	8'
Flauta travesera	8'		
Quincena	2'		
Docena y quincena	2⅔'+2'		
Nasardos (five-rank mixture)			
Nasardos (eight-rank mixture)			
Lleno (large eight-rank mixture)			

Pedal:

(in two sections, treble and bass, each of 13 keys)

Bass:		*Treble:*	
Contras	32'	Contras	2'
Contras	16'	Contras	1'
Contras	8'	Bombarda	16'
Contras en octava	4'	Clarines reales	8'
Contras	16'	Clarines	2'

Each specification may be taken as typical of a fairly large number of surviving specifications of the period 1460–1600. Many of the instruments themselves have been altered and renovated in the intervening centuries, but a few of them remain intact so that their original tone-colours can be heard and judged today. One of the most remarkable of these is in the rather ramshackle church at Oosthuizen, a small village about a mile or two from the Zuider Zee. The organ there can be taken as typical of a good parish church instrument of the sixteenth century in Northern Europe (perhaps not entirely typical of England, where organs seem to have been rather smaller). Each of the stops blends admirably with its fellows; the Quint adds a very strong reedy quality to the ensemble and the Sesquiltera produces a bell-like glitter of high harmonics. The full organ fills the church with rich, fiery sound, equal in effect to many present-day English three-manual organs, and a single stop would provide enough support for a choir of a dozen voices. Yet the total space occupied by the instrument does not exceed $5' \times 3' \times 10'$. The simple tracker-action gives the player all the subtlety of phrasing he could wish; the attack from the pipes has a sharpness comparable with the attack of an oboe reed or a martellato bow-stroke, and the whole organ is a revelation both to the player and the listener.

This seems to be the kind of sound required for the Mulliner Book, which is an anthology of English keyboard music of the mid-sixteenth century. The lighter, more transparent tone-colour corresponding to the specification of the organ at Udine is perfectly suited to the scurrying scales and clear harmonies found in the organ music of the Cavazzonis (HAM 116–18) and Andrea Gabrieli (HAM 135–6: see also 153). The German organ with its rich choice of contrasting tone-colours available on both of the manuals and the pedals, its solo reed-stops and its flutes, is adapted to the completely different style of keyboard-writing found in the German organ music of the late fifteenth and early sixteenth centuries by composers like Paumann (HAM 81), Kleber, Schlick (HAM 100–1) and Sicher. The French organ is something of a compromise between the Italian and the German styles of organ-building, and the same impression is left by the music contained in the group of organ books published by the Parisian printer, Attaingnant, in 1531; this music stands midway between the Italian and the German styles of the time.

A most important conclusion is to be drawn from this rather long discussion of Renaissance organs and their music. *Each style of composition is perfectly adapted to the particular resources at the composer's disposal*: a commonsense principle that remains true throughout the history of music, and one that is the basis of the whole of the present book. Cavazzoni's ricercars played on registrations of reeds and mixtures will sound as wrong as Schlick's plain-song fantasies played on pure Italian diapason tone. Similarly the music of Byrd, Lully, Corelli, Bach, Handel, Haydn, Mozart, Beethoven, Chopin or whom-you-please is indisseverably linked with the sonorities and styles of performance of its own time and place. If the links are snapped the music disintegrates.

THE BAROQUE ORGAN

Here again at least two national styles of organ-building must be distinguished: the Italian and the German. The Italians, like the English, remained extremely conservative: a handful of diapason stops, rising in tiers of octaves and fifths, a flute or two, and a single reed stop. Pedals were still rare, and most organs had only two manuals, one controlling the great organ rising in front of the player and above him, the other controlling the positive (known in England as the 'chair' organ) behind the organ stool. The swell box, an English invention of 1712, was still completely unknown, and all expression had to spring from nuances of phrasing, articulation, ornament and registration. These are the criteria for the stylish playing of Frescobaldi, Gibbons, Locke, Blow, Purcell and Pasquini; they are easily achieved on the lightly blown organ of the seventeenth century with its tracker-action, but not on the general run of modern instruments. In gaining the glories of diapason tone, the full swell and the solo tuba, the English

organ has lost much of the delicacy and subtlety that characterized the work of the best seventeenth-century builders; some
of their work happily is still preserved.

There is no space to discuss French and Spanish baroque
organs and organ music in any detail here; specifications and
detailed suggestions for registration may be found in the sources
of the time. The music itself is neither as fine nor as varied as
the German repertory of the same period. The long unbroken
chain of composers that began with Paix and Scheidt, continued
with Froberger and Buxtehude, and culminated in Bach can be
paralleled in no other country during the baroque period (see
HAM 190, 195–6, 215, 217, 234, 237, 249, 251). One point is
worth making, however. The German way of choosing stops
suitable for this or that piece of music was less highly organized
than the French, and one of Bach's achievements in this field
of music, as in so many others, was to take the best practice of
other countries and graft it on to the main stock of German
music. It is easy to show his familiarity with the French organ
music of his time. His Passacaglia in C minor resembles the
theme of a 'Christe eleison' by André Raison; his Fantasies
in C minor and G major resemble two organ pieces by de
Grigny and Couperin. When he was asked to draw up a
specification for the *Brustwerk* of the organ at Mühlhausen, he
seems to have modelled it on the specification of the Echo
organ in the church of St Louis des Invalides, Paris. The
logical conclusion therefore is this: that we must supplement
Bach's very laconic indications of registration or choice of
manuals by referring to the very detailed suggestions for
'Fugues graves', 'Dialogues', 'Duos', 'Fugues de mouvement'
and so on, to be found in the writings of his French contemporaries, notably de Grigny.

One specification of a German organ of the seventeenth
century must serve as an example of them all; the specification
of the organ at Steinkirchen has been chosen, since the organ
is still in its original state and has been used by Geraint Jones
for some fine and readily available recordings of Bach and other
composers, issued by English HMV.

STEINKIRCHEN (1685–91)

Great:

Quintatön	16′	Oktave	2′
Principal	8′	Gemshorn	2′
Rohrflöte	8′	Mixtur IV–VI ranks	
Oktave	4′	Sesquialtera II ranks	
Nasat	2⅔′	Trompete	8′

Manual II:

Gedackt	8′	Tertian II ranks	
Rohrflöte	4′	Scharf III–IV ranks	
Quinte	2⅔′	Krumphorn	8′
Oktave	2′	Tremulant	
Spitzflöte	2′		

Pedal:

Principal	16′	Mixtur	IV ranks
Oktave	8′	Posaune	16′
Oktave	4′	Trompete	8′
Nachthorn	2′	Kornett	2′
Rauschquint II ranks			

The organ is fairly small by comparison with the magnificent eighteenth-century instruments at Alkmaar and Gouda in Holland, or those to be found in many of the South German and Austrian churches and monasteries. Yet it provides all the contrast of sound and the clear articulation of polyphonic texture required for the music of Bach and his predecessors.

TEMPERAMENT

The subject of organs and their music has been discussed in such great detail because organs are the most long-lasting of all instruments. They can provide most useful information on the musical habits of mind of earlier times; other more fragile instruments, at the mercy of their decaying strings and reeds, cannot. Yet even on the organs that have been described in the foregoing paragraphs the music of the Renaissance and Baroque periods cannot be reproduced in exactly the form in which it was originally heard. Today all these instruments are tuned in equal temperament, which, as a tuning for practical music-making, is a complete upstart and one that was scarcely known 250 years ago.

Until the middle of the eighteenth century, ninety-five per cent of all keyboard instruments were tuned in mean-tone temperament; indeed most English organs continued to use it until the middle of the last century, and the old stops on the choir manual of the organ at Trinity College, Cambridge, remained tuned to mean-tone until about twenty or thirty years ago. This is not the place to describe all the systems of temperament, and full details will be found in Dr Lowery's book in this series.[1] For the moment it is enough to say that in the commonest mean-tone system eight major thirds (C–E, E–G♯, B♭–D, D–F♯, F–A, A–C♯, E♭–G, G–B) are exactly in tune, and a large number of common chords are consequently very much more pleasant to listen to than they are in equal temperament, in which no major third (nor any other interval except the octave, for that matter) is in tune at all. Thus mean-tone provides the player with a group of about a dozen 'central' keys in which all the important chords are very much more in tune than they are in the modern piano. In remoter keys, F♯ minor, for instance, or A♭ major, certain chords sound very disagreeable, and these chords may often include the tonic or the dominant of the keys. It is true that some of the unpleasantness can be mitigated by the use of a cunning ornament or two, and on the clavichord the player can actually control the intonation of the notes so that the problem is not so acute. Mean-tone is admittedly imperfect as a tuning for chromatic music; for diatonic music, however, it cannot be bettered, as the musicians of earlier times knew very well.

One organ of the seventeenth century, now in the castle of Frederiksborg, Denmark, is still tuned in mean-tone and the Danish organist Finn Viderø has made some very interesting discs of early music played on this instrument (issued by English HMV). In view of the availability of these discs, it seems worth while printing the specification of this organ, built by the German builder Compenius in 1616 as an instru-

[1] *The Background of Music.*

ment for chamber-music, and described in Praetorius (1615–19) as one of the finest of its kind.

Frederiksborg Castle (1616)

Manual I:

Prinzipal	8'	Gedacktquinte	2'
Gedackt	8'	Supergedackt	2⅔'
Prinzipal	4'	Zimbel III ranks	
Nachthorn	4'	Rankett	16'
Blockflöte	4'		

Manual II:

Quintade	8'	Nasat	1⅓'
Kleingedackt	4'	Zimbel II ranks	
Prinzipal	4'	Krummhorn	8'
Blockflöte	4'	Geigend Regal	4'
Gemshorn	2'		

Pedal:

Sub-bass	16'	Bauernflöte	1'
Gemshorn	8'	Sordun Bass	16'
Quintade	8'	Dulzian	4'
Querflöte	4'	Jungfern Regal	4'
Nachthorn	2'		

The important thing to realize about mean-tone is that it is not just a laboratory experiment in acoustics. It was for centuries considered to be the proper temperament for keyboard instruments, and anyone who sang or played in consort with a keyboard instrument was expected to conform to it. Rather pedantically minded musicians like Ercole Bottrigari (1594), who worked at the court of Ferrara, wrote elaborate treatises pointing out that a lute or viol (fretted in equal temperament) will not sound particularly well with a keyboard, that violinists normally play in a Pythagorean temperament which will need modifying if it is to blend with either a lute or a keyboard, and so on. The modern orchestra, with its combination of 'free' instruments (like the violin or trombone), natural-harmonic instruments (e.g. the horn and the trumpet) and equal-tempered ones (woodwind, piano, harp) would have horrified Bottrigari and his contemporaries: and the result of this hodge-podge of temperaments is often heard in the bad chord intonation of some modern orchestras.

THE VOICE

At first sight there seems no problem here, for it is easy to assume that singers have always sung in the same way. But a closer analysis reveals two separate problems: obsolete vocal tone-colours; and tone-colours that have changed.

By far the most important obsolete tone-colours, wholly unknown today but extremely fashionable during the age of the baroque, are those of the male castrato. These grown men, barbarously unmanned in their youth, retained their treble voices into their old age, using them with the maturity of technique and expression and the control of power and breathing that only comes with years of experience as a singer. Male sopranos like the incomparable Farinelli (1705–82) must have been among the finest singers not only of their own age but of all time; the eighteenth-century singing teacher Mancini wrote of Farinelli that:

> His voice was thought a marvel, because it was so perfect, so powerful, so sonorous and so rich in its extent, both in the high and the low parts of the register, that its equal has never been heard in our times. He was, moreover, endowed with a creative genius which inspired him with embellishments so new and so astonishing that no one was able to imitate them. The art of taking and keeping the breath so softly and easily that no one could perceive it began and died with him. The qualities in which he excelled were the evenness of his voice, the art of swelling its sound, the *portamento*, the union of the registers, a surprising agility, a graceful and pathetic style, and a shake as admirable as it was rare. There was no branch of the art which he did not carry to the highest pitch of perfection. . . .

A large proportion of the operatic music of the seventeenth and eighteenth centuries was written for soprano and mezzo-soprano castrati, and there is little chance of its ever being heard again in anything like its original form.

Another obsolete voice, the solo male alto or counter-tenor, has become familiar again during the last decade through the artistry of Alfred Deller. The tradition of counter-tenor singing in English cathedral choirs has never been broken since the earliest times, but solo counter-tenors of Deller's calibre must always have been rare. The voice itself seems to have been an especially English one—Purcell and Henry Lawes were both counter-tenors—and its distinctive tone-colour is an essential part of English choral music.

But both castrati and counter-tenors are highly specialized voices; what of the general run of singers? Does a tenor today make the same kind of sound as a tenor of the Renaissance? Does a Mass of Josquin's sung by a small choir today sound the same, more or less, as it did in 1515? The answer to both questions is a fairly definite 'no'. A very large number of medieval and renaissance paintings and sculptures show musicians in the act of singing, either as soloists or as members of a choir, and these provide clear evidence of the kind of tone-production favoured at the time. One of the best-known examples is van Eyck's superb 'Adoration of the Lamb'; the strained expressions on the faces of the singers are in sharp contrast with the relaxed features of the instrumentalists, and van Eyck was so scrupulous in the details of his paintings that we must assume these expressions were characteristic of the singers of his time. Now anyone can find out for himself the kind of sound that is associated with this facial expression if he stands in front of a mirror and sings. The muscles of the face and throat are tight, and the mouth is only slightly opened; the resultant sound is nasal and reedy, comparable with the contemporary taste in string and wind instruments (and compare Chaucer's Prioress: 'Ful wel she song the service divyne, Entuned in hir nose ful semely'). Just as this taste in musical instruments gave place during the sixteenth and seventeenth centuries to a taste for the subtler and sweeter colours of the violin, oboe and flute, so the vocal tone-colour changed in the same way; contemporary pictures show singers tending more and more to the modern, loose-muscled, open-throated technique of the present day. Moreover, it is very unlikely that any vibrato was used in the ensemble singing of earlier times; the few theorists who mention it condemn it.

A similar sensitiveness to the effect of vibrato is found in books dealing with solo singing or solo instrumental-playing; a vibrato was an ornament, comparable to a mordent, a trill, a *messa di voce* or a slide, and it is to be used no more and no less frequently than the other graces. In ensemble music it is to be used only with the greatest discretion.[1] To sing a medieval or Renaissance motet in a truly authentic way a choir should presumably aim at the kind of sound produced by the choir of Dijon cathedral (some of their discs have been issued by English HMV). It would certainly seem that the individual polyphonic lines of a complex work are heard at their most distinct only when (a) all the singers in the choir use virtually no vibrato; (b) the sound-quality of the voices approximates to the hard sinewy tone of the Dijon choir (and indeed of most French solo singers).

VOCAL ENSEMBLES

Repeated references in, for instance, the establishment books of the Chapel Royal or the diaries of the Sistine Chapel make it clear that the minimum number of singers required for a full choral service in the sixteenth century was from twelve to sixteen. Some works admittedly seem to have been designed for solo voices—the three-part Masses of Ludford, for instance; the sections carefully marked 'duo' or 'gimel' in much music of the fifteenth century; or the organa of Pérotin and his contemporaries—but these are exceptions, and they are usually characteristic of medieval taste rather than that of the Renaissance. To decide the maximum size is more difficult, and in any case this was probably governed by the amount of money the owner of the choir could afford to spend on keeping it up. On special occasions like the festivities of the Field of the Cloth of Gold, or the magnificent wedding celebrations of the Medici family, the records of the time show that very large numbers of singers and players took part.

Secular music is another matter altogether. Pictures of

[1] And in solo music. The incessant vibrato which has so regrettably infected nine out of every ten singers of the present day could not be obtained with the methods of breath-control taught by the finest eighteenth- and nineteenth-century singing teachers. The evidence of early recordings shows that even fifty years ago it was used with the utmost care (though the tremolo seems to have been rather more common than it is today), and it is one of the greatest disfigurements of modern musical performance.

fifteenth- and sixteenth-century singers singing chansons, frottolas and madrigals always show very small groups of solo performers, not choirs. A certain amount of supporting evidence comes from the musical sources of the time. Polyphonic music, whether for instruments or for voices, was set down on paper for the performers in one of two forms: either with all the parts laid out on the open page, not in score but one after another (the so-called choir-book); or else in individual part-books, one to each part. No part-books written earlier than 1460 or so are now known to exist, and it is indeed very probable that they were an invention of the mid-fifteenth century.[1]

Choir-books for sacred music are often very large and written in very large notes, and many pictures exist showing a group of a dozen men and boys grouped round a lectern holding a single book of this kind.[2] But secular choir-books were smaller, and they cannot be used by more than three or four performers at once. And music books of all kinds were so extremely expensive in earlier times that very few musicians could have afforded to buy two copies of the same work. Inventories of the musical libraries of cathedrals, clubs and private persons never show more than one copy of any particular set of pieces, and there is no reason to distrust evidence of this kind.

The conclusion is inescapable. The vast sixteenth-century secular repertory of English, French, German, Italian and Spanish instrumental music and song (a representative selection in HAM) was designed as chamber music, to be performed by

[1] But the whole question is a very delicate one. Most of the surviving manuscripts of the Middle Ages show none of the signs of use that one would expect to find in performer's music. There are no dog-eared pages, no pencilled corrections, no cues, no finger-marks, no spots of candle-grease; all of which is rather odd. One is forced to conclude that these manuscripts were either presentation copies or else records of repertory, and that they were not material actually used for performance. When literacy is rare, memories are good; and it may well have been the custom for much music to be learned by heart and so performed. Moreover, music used for performance wears out quickly; what there was in earlier times was probably used until it fell to pieces and was thrown away.

[2] Here again the scholar is disturbed by one or two points. For instance, the vocal parts for boys might be expected to be found at the bottom of the page, instead of which, in surviving manuscripts, they are almost without exception at the top. This strengthens the suggestion that these splendid books were for reference rather than for everyday use.

one or possibly two musicians to a part. It is perhaps a little odd that though present-day musicians would be outraged at the suggestion that Mozart's string quartets should be played orchestrally, they cheerfully accept sixteenth-century chamber music blown up several times larger than life by a choir or a string band.

INSTRUMENTAL ENSEMBLES

Orchestral music as such can scarcely be said to exist before the latter part of the seventeenth century. The operatic and theatre music of Carissimi, Purcell and Lully was written for fairly small ensembles and is so performed today; but this is not concert music, which begins with the concerto grosso of Corelli and his contemporaries and continues its triumphant course down to the present time. Until very recently the earlier part of this orchestral repertory was usually performed in a hopelessly anachronistic way.

The two main faults have been those of the size of the ensemble, and its layout on the concert platform. In a concerto grosso, the group of soloists should contrast with the ripieno group in which each part is played by two or three players. Each group should have its own continuo instrument (Handel's concerti grossi were issued with two continuo parts, though the nineteenth-century editors of his complete works suppressed one of these altogether); there is no need to restrict these to harpsichords. The title pages of the time suggest that the continuo may be played on a harpsichord, a spinet, a harp, an organ or an arch-lute; and if a present-day concert programme contains only a single work of this kind, it seems a very extravagant thing to hire a harpsichord and a harpsichordist when a harpist can do the job instead. The two groups of players, soloists and ripienists, must be separated on the concert platform as they would have been in the eighteenth century; this element of space is inherent in the form, and it derives ultimately from the dispositions of the performers used in St. Mark's, Venice, and elsewhere at the beginning of the seventeenth century. The two or more separate groups of voices and instruments used in the works of the Gabrielis were placed in different galleries of the churches and cathedrals in which they were performed,[1] each ensemble having its own conductor and continuo-player (who were usually one and the same person). To set out all these groups on the platform, massed into one large body of performers, is to strip the music of one of its dimensions.

The later eighteenth-century symphony is commonly treated as insensitively as the earlier concerto grosso. Again there are the same two points to consider: layout, and size. Engravings and other illustrations of eighteenth-century orchestras make it clear that the usual concert layout placed the first and second violins on opposite sides of the orchestra, with the double-basses and cellos in the centre of the platform, close to the leader and the continuo-player. The sound-pattern from an orchestral array of this kind is utterly different from the sound-pattern produced by the most commonly used orchestral array of our own time; and there can be no doubt that the orchestration used by the early symphonists was devised to make use of the antiphonal effects of the violins, pivoted about the deeper notes of the bass instruments and the harmonies of the violas and the continuo. The blend of the strings is of course better in the modern orchestral layout; but the eighteenth century was perfectly free to adopt such a layout if it had wanted to, and the fact that it did not is very important.

Most modern conductors contemptuously ignore the eighteenth century's clearly expressed views on the proper size and composition of an orchestra. If these views were merely derived from the establishment lists of this or that court orchestra, they might legitimately be attacked on the grounds that the composition of a court orchestra was largely governed by the amount of money available for it. But the evidence of the establishment lists is amply confirmed by the many writers of the period who wrote books and essays on good taste in music. Nor can the evidence be brushed aside on the grounds that the balance of sound between various individual instruments has changed during the last century

[1]There is abundant evidence for this in the writings of the time, not only for Venice but also for Rome, Milan, Salzburg and elsewhere.

or two. The individual sounds have changed, it is true, but the relative strengths of the instruments have not; as the eighteenth-century oboe or clarinet is to the eighteenth-century violin, so is the twentieth-century oboe or clarinet to the twentieth-century violin, roughly speaking. And this exercise in proportion is no mere fancy plucked from the air; it is based on considerable experience of hearing both old and new instruments played in ensembles by competent players.

Here are some typical eighteenth-century orchestras, with the relevant parts of a twentieth-century symphony orchestra for comparison.

	ORCHESTRAS				
	Eighteenth century				Twentieth century
	small	medium	large	very large	
1st violins	2–3	4	6	9–10	12
2nd violins	2–3	4	6	9–10	10
violas	1	2	3	5	8
cellos	1	2	3	4	8
double-basses	1	2	2–3	4	6
oboes	1	2	4	4	2
flutes	–	2	4	4	2
bassoons	1	2	3	3	2
horns	–	1	2	2–4	4
continuo	1	1	2	2–3	–
trumpets	–	–	2	2	2
timpani	–	–	1	1	1

Some extremely important conclusions may be drawn from this table. (1) In all the eighteenth-century orchestras the violins are equally divided into firsts and seconds; in the modern orchestra the firsts predominate, though only slightly. (2) For every fifteen violins, the eighteenth-century orchestra had ten violas, cellos and double-basses; the modern orchestra has fifteen. The modern orchestra is bottom-heavy, in fact. (3) For every fifteen violins, the eighteenth-century orchestra had six of each woodwind instrument; the modern orchestra has two.[1] (4) For every fifteen violins the eighteenth-century orchestra had two continuo instruments; the modern orchestra has none. Only one of these instruments was essential for the task of controlling and directing the ensemble; any others must therefore have been used because the sound was liked, not because there was no way of doing without it.

PITCH

From about 1600 to 1820 or so, the internationally used pitch for instrumental music remained fairly steady at rather more than a semitone below the one in use today ($a' = 440$). Naturally enough there were local deviations from this generally accepted standard. The tuning fork was not invented until 1711, and there was in any case no particular reason for enforcing the international use of a single exactly determined pitch, so that no one tried to do so. Certain instruments were traditionally tuned higher or lower than normal. Music for cornetts, for instance, sounded rather more than a tone higher than its written pitch would suggest, and organ music rather more than a semitone higher. But most instruments used the low pitch which is still found in folk instruments like the bagpipe and the pipe-and-tabor.

The implications of these facts are considerable, though they are not easy to put into practice. They are specially relevant to music involving a combination of voices and instruments; thus Bach's Mass in B minor ought properly to be performed in B flat minor or even in A minor; the opening movement of *Messiah* should be in D sharp minor; Beethoven's ninth symphony should be in D flat minor or even in C (which would make the solo and chorus parts much less of a strain to sing). Obviously transpositions of this kind will sometimes be quite impossible to carry out, since they may make certain passages quite unplayable on instruments using today's standard tuning. But many highly publicized attempts at producing authentic versions of this or that piece of early

[1] A few exceptional orchestras had more strings than this table would suggest; see Emily Anderson's edition of *Mozart's Letters*, vol. III, p. 1076.

music have quite ignored the question of restoring it to its proper pitch, though there seems little doubt that when such transpositions are possible they should be carried out.

ACOUSTICAL SURROUNDINGS

Here is another vast subject which it is impossible to treat in the detail it deserves. But even a superficial study shows that early composers were very aware of the effect on their music of the surroundings in which it was to be performed, and that they deliberately shaped their music accordingly.

Musical acoustics may be roughly divided into 'resonant', 'room', and 'outdoor'. Plainsong is resonant music; so is the harmonic style of Léonin (HAM 29) and Pérotin (HAM 31), designed for solo singers and constructed of long chains of freely moving counterpoints stretched between points of repose. Pérotin's music, in fact, is perfectly adapted to the acoustics of the highly resonant cathedral (Notre Dame, Paris) for which it was written. The intricate sophisticated rhythms and harmonies of the fourteenth-century *ars nova* (HAM 45, 47-8) are room-music; pieces written in the broader style of the fifteenth century (HAM 63-4, 66) are resonant music. No instrument is specified, as a rule, in the manuscripts of keyboard music by Elizabethan and Jacobean composers, but some of it is clearly resonant music and therefore most suited to the organ, while another part is as clearly room-music for the harpsichord, virginals or clavichord. Gabrieli's music for brass consort is resonant, written for the cathedral of St. Mark's; music for brass consort by Hassler or Matthew Locke is open-air music, using quite a different style from the same composers' music for stringed instruments, designed to be played indoors. Purcell distinguished in style between the music he wrote for Westminster Abbey and the music he wrote for the Chapel Royal; both styles differ from that of his theatre music, written for performance in completely 'dead' surroundings. The forms used by Mozart and Haydn in their chamber and orchestral music are identical; but the details of style (counterpoint, ornamentation, rhythm, the layout of chords, and the rate at which harmonies change) will vary according to whether they are writing room-music, concert-music, or street-music.

Such a list could be extended indefinitely, though it is doubtful whether the list would include all the composers of the present day. Our own age has grown very insensitive to nuances of this kind; but there is plenty of written evidence (quite apart from the evidence of the music itself) to show that they were taken very seriously in earlier times. One example will serve for many; in the middle of a tedious Latin discussion of his proposed new notation for music the obscure seventeenth-century musician J. van der Elst (1657) breaks off to write three or four paragraphs full of common sense about the performing of vocal polyphony in a resonant building. 'Sound,' he says,

'gradually dwindles when it is perceived from a distance, just as the columns of a long portico stretching straight ahead seem to draw together little by little and, though they are in fact widely spaced, appear to be joined together. Similarly, when several notes are set to a single syllable, each must be articulated distinctly and with attention to detail, lest to anyone hearing them at a distance they seemed blurred and little more than a continuous up-and-down humming. Melodies sung in a clear style, with this well-defined separation of the notes, reach the ear of the listener some way away in a smooth distinct flow.'

Many present-day choral performances, in highly resonant buildings, of works designed for more intimate surroundings would be the better for van der Elst's advice.

Similarly, it is often forgotten that the average seventeenth- or eighteenth-century music room was acoustically very different from those of the present day, and many gramophone records and broadcasts of baroque and classical chamber music are consequently far too dry. An eighteenth-century music-room contained far less furniture than a twentieth-century one, the walls of the room were often panelled or painted and the wooden floors were polished and uncarpeted. The resonance of the room was therefore high and chamber music had a lustre which was, and should be, an integral part of its texture.

CHAPTER IV

EXTEMPORIZATION

EXTEMPORIZATION of one kind and another played a very large part in early music, but during the last two centuries or so it has fallen increasingly out of fashion. It is probably no mere coincidence that musical notation during the same period has enmeshed the performer in an ever-closing net of precise and tyrannical directions. Composers like Stravinsky and Schönberg leave the interpreter no freedom whatever; every nuance of dynamic, tempo, phrasing, rhythm and expression is rigidly prescribed, and the performer is reduced to the abject status of a pianola or a gramophone. Indeed the ultimate stage in this freezing process has perhaps been reached in a gramophone disc itself. A disc of Mr X conducting the Blanktown Symphony Orchestra in a performance of a work he wrote especially for them is rapidly acquiring the status, if not of the Mosaic Tablets, at least of the Authorized Version.

This progressive annihilation of the performer's share in the creation of a piece of music is an alarming phenomenon and one that has never occurred before in the whole history of music, European and non-European. Expelled with a pitchfork, nature nevertheless has a habit of coming back: the virtuoso performer or conductor now takes the stage, famous for *his* reading of Bach or Beethoven. He, too, is a new phenomenon in his twentieth-century version, for he regards the written notes as unalterable (or virtually so), no matter how impetuously he scatters them with arbitrarily chosen tempi, dynamics and phrasings. The virtuoso performers of the nineteenth and earlier centuries were a different breed of men altogether. At their best they regarded the composer's own text as a challenge to their inventiveness and resource, a basic canvas to be embellished here and there with variations, roulades and divisions. Ferdinand David, for instance, was greatly admired some eighty years ago for the skill with which he introduced varied repeats in the performance of chamber music by Mozart and Haydn.

This attitude towards the composer and his work was often encouraged by the composer himself, and the performer could legitimately feel that it was not only his right but also his duty to make a substantial creative contribution of his own to the music he was performing. Many of the greatest composers of earlier times were famous as extemporizers, and very often their contemporary reputation rested far more on their extemporizations than on their written compositions. Those who heard Liszt and Chopin play wrote in admiration of the elegant way in which they varied their music from performance to performance, adding new passage-work and revising the layout of the accompanying chords. '[Chopin's] finest compositions were but a reflex and echo of his improvisations. When he played, the left hand was steady, distinct, and in perfect time; the right hand was independent' (this is true rubato).

C. P. E. Bach was the greatest keyboard extemporizer of his time, and his 'free fantasies' (HAM 296) and 'sonatas with varied repeats' were intended, like those of his contemporary F. W. Rust, as models of how to do the same sort of thing extempore. The cadenza in a concerto or a sonata was an opportunity for the player to improvise some exciting fantasy on the themes of the movement; Mozart's cadenzas to his concertos were designed as models, not as obligatory insertions. Like Beethoven, he was a superb extemporizer; Holmes (1828) writes of Mozart's clever modulation and grace and his use of canon, and of Beethoven's fire and energy, in extempore playing. When Moscheles, Thalberg and Mendelssohn played Bach's D minor triple concerto on three pianos at a London concert in 1844, each player in turn interpolated a long extemporized cadenza, Mendelssohn's being judged the most apt and elegant, and Thalberg's the poorest. The insertion of such cadenzas was no novelty; it was taken as a matter of course. Bach, Handel, Couperin, Rameau, Corelli and many others published superb examples of how to embellish repeats or to improvise variations, and any eighteenth-century player who played the first part of a sarabande, say, and then repeated it note for note would have been thought a very dull dog.

This liking for skilled (and even unskilled) extemporization seems to increase rather than to diminish as we travel back in musical history. Throughout the seventeenth and eighteenth centuries any would-be conductor, organist or keyboard-player was expected to be able to play fluently from a figured bass in ensemble music. The seventeenth-century amateur of the bass-viol taught himself to extemporize divisions on a ground bass, either by himself or in consort with others, all the players joining together finally

> in a Thunderous Strain of *Quick* Division; with which they may conclude; or else with a Strain of slow and sweet Notes, according as may best sute the circumstance of time and place.
> I have known this kind of *Extemporary* Musick, sometimes (when it was performed by Hands accustomed to Play together) pass off with greater applause, than those Divisions which had been most studiously composed.
>
> Simpson (1667)

And Bacon hits upon a happy analogy:

> The *Division* and *Quavering*, which please so much in *Musick*, have an agreement with the *Glittering* of Light; As the *Moonbeames* playing upon a Wave.
>
> (*Sylva Sylvarum*, 1626)

Whole movements were sometimes left to the players to make up on the spot. Thus in many of Handel's organ concertos phrases like 'Adagio ad libitum' are found, and on occasion there is even room for a whole fugue. This tradition of extemporizing slow movements is no doubt the explanation of the two chords which separate the first and second movements of Bach's third Brandenburg concerto; as Tovey pointed out long ago, these are quite meaningless in themselves. But if it be supposed that a slow movement was to be interpolated at this point, perhaps extemporized by the leader, the continuo-player and a string bass, then the chords make sense; for they are clearly designed to lead back from a slow movement in the relative minor towards the home key of the 12/8 finale. In some recent performances of this concerto various movements from Bach's sonatas for violin and harpsichord or violin and continuo have been used for this purpose, and one or two of them are particularly fortunate choices. Certainly something of the kind is required; to play the chords with great feeling and exquisite tone as though they constituted in themselves a whole slow movement is as absurd as to try to pronounce a comma as though it were a paragraph. The chords are a punctuation mark and nothing more.

The sixteenth century was as fond of extemporization as the seventeenth century, and surviving treatises on the subject suggest that the art was very highly developed. A sixteenth-century quartet, vocal or instrumental, professional or amateur, prided themselves on the skill with which they could elaborate a madrigal, motet or fantasy. Palestrina's music as it was then performed in an important Roman church or chapel bore little resemblance to the text as we see it printed today; for one thing, it was usually accompanied by the organ—softly, to be sure, but nevertheless accompanied—and for another, the leading singer of each part would from time to time extemporize an elaborate roulade. These roulades were at their most elaborate in cadences (hence the word 'cadenza'), and their use dates back at least to the time of Josquin. But roulades of this kind—divisions on a written-out part—were perhaps not as significant as another practice of the time, the extemporizing of a tune in counterpoint to a given canto fermo. As early as 1390 the 'Monk of Salzburg' expected his composition pupils to be able to extemporize a counterpoint to a well-known tune, and the whole of the composition teaching of the fifteenth and sixteenth centuries was based on the same technique. Morley's *Plain and Easy Introduction*, for example, begins by teaching a pupil the rudiments of music and sight-reading; part II of the book is concerned with what Morley and his contemporaries called 'descant', that is to say, improvised vocal counterpoint; and finally the pupil is taught how to compose on paper. The seventeenth- and eighteenth-century composition student also learned to compose by means of extemporizing, though for him it was not so much a question of improvising counterpoints as of improvising harmonies above a figured bass. But the late eighteenth-century pedants who turned counterpoint and harmony into 'paper work' have much to answer for; they forced the ear to abdicate in favour of the eye, and they broke the links of extemporization that in all earlier times had held composer, performer, and listener in a single musical chain.

This survey of extemporization and its importance in the musical life of earlier times could be extended almost without limit, for it can be taken to embrace all music from the organum of the tenth century to nineteenth-century techniques of performance. Enough has already been said to show that any picture of this music will be impossibly distorted unless and until it is realized how big was the part that extemporization played. Many of the techniques used have been lost, and some of them need not be mourned. For instance, it is rather doubtful whether Palestrina's music was really heard at its best smothered in whirligig vocal ornament, and certain of Palestrina's own contemporaries and successors were critical of its use. Cerone (1613) wrote that 'when all the performers extemporize divisions at once, one would think one was in a synagogue or among a flock of geese'. But other lost techniques of improvisation have impoverished the musical community, one of the greatest losses perhaps being that of improvised continuo-playing.[1] There are at most three or four keyboard-players in the whole of Great Britain who can be relied upon to play from a figured bass fluently and with a sense of style. The majority of so-called continuo-players can do no more than plod through the dull, relentless succession of four-note chords which is all that most editors see fit to set before them, and this is no way to provide the spirit, the drive, and the variety that should come from a continuo-player who knows how to make up his part as he goes along. As Geminiani (c. 1745) wrote:

With Respect to the *Thorough Bass* on the *Harpsichord*, it has been my particular Aim to observe a great variety of Harmony and Movements, which two Things are most agreeable to the Nature of that Instrument; and have given the following short

[1]This was not restricted to harmony instruments. Holmes (1828) writes of the way in which the English cellist, Lindley, used to accompany recitatives at the London opera house elegantly and fancifully, with brilliant arpeggio chords and delicately sustained notes.

Rules, for the use of those who desire to accompany in a good Taste. They must be sure to place the Chords between both Hands, in such a Manner as to produce (by passing from one Chord to another) at once both an agreeable Harmony and Melody. Sometimes playing many Chords, and at other Times few, for our Delight arises from the Variety. Whenever the Upper Part stops, and the Bass continues, He who accompanies must make some Melodious Variation on the same Harmony, in order to awaken the Imagination of the Performer, whether he Sings or Plays, and at the same Time to give Pleasure to the Hearer. . . . In accompanying grave Movements, he should make use of the *Acciachature*, for these rightly placed, have a wonderful Effect; and now and then should touch the several Notes of the Chord lightly one after another, to keep the Harmony alive. . . . Particular Care should be taken to touch the Keys of the Instrument delicately, otherwise the Accompanyment of the *Drum* would be as grateful as that of the *Harpsichord*. He who accompanies should by no means play the Part of the Person who Sings or Plays, unless with an Intention to instruct or affront him. . . . To conclude, I must beg Leave to affirm that he who has no other Qualities than that of playing the Notes in Time, and placing the Figures, as well as he can, is but a wretched Accompanyer.

Geminiani's remarks gain even more weight when we remember that on many occasions he was accompanied by Handel himself. William Babell published a collection of pieces and continuos by Handel written out as Handel played them, and this collection completely confirms what Geminiani has to say. And those who heard Bach's continuo-playing wrote of it in terms that echo Geminiani's almost word for word.

It is not necessary to rely merely on what the eighteenth century had to say about good continuo-playing in order to discover its importance. The present century is beginning to rediscover what the eighteenth century knew perfectly well: that, as Couperin (1716) said, the continuo is the foundation of the building and, though little of it may be noticeable, it nevertheless supports the whole musical structure. Or, to quote C. P. E. Bach

'the emptiness of a performance without this accompanying instrument is, unfortunately, made apparent to us far too often. . . .

No piece can be well performed without some form of keyboard accompaniment. Even in heavily scored works, such as operas performed out of doors, where no one would think that the harpsichord could be heard, its absence can certainly be felt.'

A team consisting of an experienced continuo-player, a know-ledgeable leader (rare) and a good continuo cellist (rarer still) can control a performance of baroque music at least as well as some conductors and rather better than most. And ex-temporized continuo-playing is not only extremely exhilarating both to the player and to the listener; it also trains the player to be simultaneously quick in reading, thinking, listening and acting. But it is an art that takes a long time to master. Only the rudiments can be learned from a book and there are shamefully few players who are qualified to teach it.

DIVISIONS

Here again there is all the difference in the world between a performer who has learnt how to extemporize his own ornaments, and one who merely executes those written down on paper for him by someone else. Many eighteenth-century books and manuscripts provide examples of how Corelli or Geminiani ornamented a slow movement, or how Mrs Arne sang this or that da capo in some Handel oratorio or opera. But it is preposterous for any performer of the present day to spend time learning these ornaments note for note in order to repro-duce them on the concert platform with an air that is as dogged as it is self-conscious, and no editor or scholar ought to ask them to do it on the pretext that the result will be the first authentic performance since seventeen hundred and something. It will not be. The music will lack all the spontaneity and brio that spring from true extemporization; the performer will feel embarrassed; the editor will acquire a specious reputation for scholarliness; and the audience will be either deluded or amused. No old music deserves such treatment.

If it is impossible for performers either to learn how to extemporize or at least how to give the impression that they are extemporizing, then let the music be performed as it stands. There is plenty of evidence to show that many seventeenth- and eighteenth-century critics preferred it this way:

> *I shall desire . . . you would do yourselves and me the right to play plain, not* Tearing *them in pieces with* Division, (*an old custome of our* Country Fidlers *and now under the title of* A la mode *endevored to be introduced*). . . .
>
> Locke (1656)

> Let [the solo violinist in a concerto] avoid all extravagant Decorations, since every Attempt of this Kind must utterly destroy whatever Passion the Composer may have designed to express.
>
> Avison (1752)

> Therefore it may reasonably be supposed, that those Contrivances, which have been the result of Time and Thought, are not very likely to be improved by any Performance *extempore*.
>
> Avison (1756)

> We have another instance of the little regard paid to the ultimate end of Music, the affecting the heart and passions, in the universally allowed practice of making a long flourish at the close of a song, and sometimes at other periods of it. In this the performer is left at liberty to shew the utmost compass of his throat and execution, and all that is required, is, that he should conclude in the proper key; the performer accordingly takes this opportunity of shewing the audience the extent of his abilities, by the most fantastical and unmeaning extravagance of execution. The disgust which this gives to some, and the surprise which it excites in all the audience, breaks the tide of passion in the soul, and destroys all the effect which the composer has been labouring to produce.
>
> Gregory (1766)

> [I am unable to describe] the encompassing a Note with frippery flourishes that prevent the real sound from meeting the ear . . . [or] the filling up an Interval with something composed of a *slide* and a *shout* by which means there is no Interval at all . . . [or] Cadences with, for ever, a concluding shake . . . and every shake with precisely the same turn after it.
>
> Jackson (1791)

CHAPTER V

STYLE IN THE EIGHTEENTH CENTURY

EACH period of musical history will present certain cardinal problems of style to the student of interpretation; these problems may be notational conventions, which will mislead the performer unless he has been warned of their existence, or conventions of performance, concerned with dynamics, articulation, sonorities, phrasing, and so on. In the next chapters of this book some of these problems will be examined in the light of contemporary evidence, and some suggestions will be made as to their possible solution.

OPTIONAL INSTRUMENTATION

All symphonies, overtures, concertos, suites, serenades, divertimentos and other orchestral music of the eighteenth century were sold to the public in sets of separate parts, and full scores were scarcely ever published. For the sake of cheapness the number of parts in a set was kept as low as possible; separate parts for woodwind, horns, or trumpets and drums were seldom likely to be required often enough to warrant the expense of engraving them, and quite frequently they were only issued in manuscript or even regarded as omissible altogether in performance. Innumerable title-pages of the period bear remarks like 'double-basses, trumpets and timpani will greatly add to the effect of this piece; those who require parts for them should get in touch with M. Lallemand, the copyist of the Opera House' (J. F. Rebel, *c.* 1750) and 'Six symphonies in four parts, with optional parts for horns, by M. Stamitz. The horn parts are on sale separately' (*c.* 1755). Surviving sets of printed parts, which are themselves fairly rare today, seldom if ever include these optional parts for trumpets or drums; and a full score prepared from them will therefore give quite a misleading impression of how the work sounded when performed by the largest orchestras of the time, even though it may adequately represent a small-scale performance.

The violin parts were often intended to be played by oboes as well;[1] sometimes the only indication of this device is, as in some of Handel's concertos, the sudden indication 'senza oboi' in a trio to a minuet. Moreover an orchestra that included oboes automatically included at least one bassoon. No separate part for the bassoon would be printed, since the bassoonist would in general be playing the printed bass-line in unison with the left hand of the continuo-player and the string basses. But if the oboes at any point had a solo passage to themselves, accompanied merely by the thorough-bass line, it was taken as a matter of course that in performance this bass-line would be played for the moment by the bassoon and the harpsichord, the string basses being silent. The same treatment of the bass-line was expected when the solo instruments were flutes or clarinets (which in any case were then regarded as more or less interchangeable with oboes) and also for solo horns (HAM 295, bars 5–9). Many modern editors seem to be quite unaware of the existence of this convention, and as a result many standard editions of the present-day orchestral repertory (Mozart, Haydn, Handel, Bach) are faulty in their treatment of the woodwind writing.

Viola parts are often lacking, too, but this does not mean that violas were not used. At the time it was understood that when there was no separate part for them the violas doubled the bass-line an octave higher than it was written (e.g. HAM 295). Quantz (1752) indeed warned the players that their part must never be allowed to cross above the top line of the music, and that where necessary they must play in unison with the bass (see HAM 294 for viola parts that are tied to the bass almost throughout the movement). Orchestration of this kind may seem very slipshod to us, but the eighteenth century knew what it was doing. If the basic harmonic background to the music is

[1]See, for instance, Boyce's directions to the copyist in his autograph score of *Saul and Jonathan* (Royal College of Music): 'The Hautboys with the Violins excepting when they go too high, then take them 8 notes lower for a bar or two as you find occasion. Observe the same if they get too low.'

being provided by the continuo instruments, then the contra-puntal lines must be made to sound as clear as possible; and the bass-line will gain in clarity by the addition of the viola tone, just as an organ pedal line will sound clearer with a 4' stop added to the normal 8' and 16' stops. Eighteenth-century organ-builders provided the player with a selection of stops of this kind on quite small instruments as well as on large ones, and even the smallest eighteenth-century orchestra included a viola for the same reason.

Horns, like trumpets and drums, were luxuries in the eighteenth-century orchestra, but when they were available they were used. If there were no parts for them these could be quickly supplied by the orchestral director (who was usually the continuo-player), for the limited scale of the natural horn or trumpet set severe limits on the kind of music it usually played (see HAM 259, 295). As for the timpanist, his part could easily be improvised on the spot from a low trumpet part; Bach's timpani parts are usually almost identical with those for the third trumpet, who was seldom expected to be able to do more than hop up and down on the tonic and dominant. The same is true of many of the existing timpani parts in the music of Handel, Mozart and Haydn, and it is easy to supply missing parts (e.g. in HAM 259) making use of the evidence provided by those which do exist.

To sum up:

(1) The absence of a part specifically labelled 'oboe' or 'viola' or 'trumpet' or 'bassoon' or 'continuo' does not in the least imply that these instruments were not used if they were available.

(2) The three woodwind tone-colours are often interchange-able in the orchestral music of the second half of the century, and the judicious conductor may like to vary his orchestration accordingly. Composers of the time preferred to use oboes in the fast movements and flutes or clarinets in the slow move-ments.

(3) Whenever one or more wind instruments are used the

bass-line should be strengthened by a bassoon. Wind instruments playing solo passages should be accompanied by a wind bass, the string basses being silent. Wind parts were normally doubled, except in solo or obbligato passages.

(4) If there is no part for violas, they should double the bass-line in the upper octave, dropping down in unison with it whenever they would otherwise pass above the main treble tune.

(5) Horns and trumpets are often interchangeable, though timpani were used with horns only in England. If horns and trumpets are available and there is no music for them to play, additional parts for them may need to be composed; these will be anachronistic unless they make use only of the notes of the natural, valveless trumpet or horn. Timpani parts will more or less double those for the second or third trumpets. It would be quite in accordance with the practice of the time if parts of this kind were added to the earlier symphonies of Mozart and Haydn. Similarly, parts for side-drums and cymbals should be added to marches and other military music.

(6) For any works lacking the fineness of inner texture of the later symphonies of Mozart and Haydn at least one continuo instrument will be essential in order to make the music cohere. Works for double orchestra will naturally require two.

(7) In the eighteenth century an orchestral work could be played by many different ensembles ranging from a string quartet and a harpsichord to a symphony orchestra of forty or fifty players. But a certain fixed balance of sound between string, woodwind, brass and keyboard instruments was always preserved, and the same variety and care for balance should characterize present-day performances.

(8) These are suggestions rather than rules. The conductor of an amateur orchestra will find them a useful way of providing parts for instruments that might otherwise have nothing to do. The professional conductor and the editor may find them at best stimulating, and at worst tiresome and lacking in taste. But since they represent the very practical attitude of the

eighteenth century towards its own music they cannot be rejected out of hand.

HARPSICHORD AND CLAVICHORD VERSUS PIANO

The tone-colour of a late eighteenth-century harpsichord was not very different from that of a contemporary fortepiano, but the tone-colours of their modern descendants are very unlike one another. A Viennese fortepiano and a Kirkman harpsichord are more or less interchangeable, and similar though not identical styles of writing were used for both; thus in C. P. E. Bach's double concerto for harpsichord and fortepiano, the idiom of the one instrument does not differ much from the idiom of the other. But this concerto will sound fairly unpleasant when it is played on a modern grand piano teamed with a modern harpsichord, for the sounds of the two instruments battle against, rather than contrast with, each other. In a word, much eighteenth-century keyboard music sounded equally well when played on any contemporary keyboard instrument, but the sounds of their modern descendants have diverged so greatly that this is no longer true. Consequently some attempt must be made to discover which instrument the composer had particularly in mind when he wrote.

Leaving aside for the moment the question of clavichord music, it is clear that throughout Europe the harpsichord was decidedly preferred to the piano until about 1770 or so. During the next twenty years the piano steadily gained in favour and the harpsichord as steadily declined, and from 1790 onwards the harpsichord was regarded as outworn and obsolete (Haydn wrote at the time that he had grown quite out of the habit of using it). Generally speaking, therefore, the harpsichord is the proper instrument to use for music written before 1770, the piano for music written after 1790. Haydn's first nineteen sonatas are harpsichord music (though in his own catalogue of his works he later listed no. 18 as for piano). The first crescendo mark occurs in no. 29, and the first perdendosi in no. 34; neither of these effects could be obtained on the traditional harpsichord of his own time unless it was fitted with a Venetian swell, yet both were published in 1778 as music 'per cembalo', that is to say, for the harpsichord. But these pieces, like all the sonatas from no. 20 onwards, show an increasing use of idioms which are essentially pianistic, and modern performances of them unquestionably call for the use of a piano. Similarly the evidence of the titles of Mozart's early sonatas and concertos, as well as of their texture and the places in which they were first performed, often betrays the fact that they were written for the harpsichord, not the piano; thus K. 271 is headed in the autograph 'Concerto per il Clavicembalo', and most of the works he wrote in Paris or for Parisian performers during the 1770s are for harpsichord. The distinction in style between the harpsichord music and the piano music of Mozart, Haydn and their contemporaries ought to be preserved as far as possible even when all of it is played indiscriminately on the piano.

Clavichord music is less of a problem, since its expressive nuances and delicately graded dynamics can be played only on a clavichord or, less perfectly, on a piano. It has been pointed out in Chapter III that the clavichord, not the harpsichord, is the true ancestor of the piano, and that the techniques and styles of composition and performance appropriate to the clavichord and the fortepiano were for many years very similar.[1] C. P. E. Bach's astonishing sonatas, fantasias and rondos were published for 'connoisseurs and amateurs' of the clavichord and fortepiano, and very few of them are suited to the harpsichord. But a good deal of his earlier keyboard music was very definitely written for the harpsichord, making full use of its distinctive idioms, its terraced dynamics and its elegant brilliance. No player of the harpsichord and clavichord will have any difficulty in deciding which instrument should be used for any particular piece, but the following general hints may perhaps be found helpful.

[1]The late eighteenth-century composer, Reichardt, pointed out that 'the harpsichord cannot receive the smallest degree of soul, expression and feeling save from the hand of him who knows how to animate the clavichord; . . . he who once masters this instrument plays the harpsichord quite differently from those who never touch a clavichord'. Virdung (1511) wrote that once one had learnt how to play the clavichord it was easy to learn how to play the organ, the harpsichord, the virginals, and all other keyboard instruments. See also N. Broder, 'Mozart and the Clavier', *MQ* (1941).

	Harpsichord	*Clavichord and fortepiano*
texture	fairly constant (HAM 308)	ever-changing
dynamics	terraced (*f* and *p*) infrequent changes	carefully graded constant changes (HAM 296)
cresc., dim.	none (HAM 303)	many (HAM 304)
repeated notes	unslurred	slurred and dotted (HAM 296)
form	binary, variation, suite (HAM 280, 284, 302)	sonata, rondo (HAM 297)
style	classical, severe (HAM 308)	romantic, sentimental (HAM 288)
use in ensemble	very frequent	for the clavichord: almost unknown; for the fortepiano: fairly common (HAM 304)

With the music of the composers of the first half of the eighteenth century the matter is more delicate. The dividing lines between the styles suitable for the various instruments were less sharply defined and preferences were less clearly expressed. Certain pointers exist, nevertheless, and on the basis of these some fairly shrewd and well-founded guesses may be made.

Thus any piece or set of pieces which the composer intended 'to develop a cantabile style of playing' (e.g. Bach's Three-part Inventions, which are so described in the composer's own preface) are essentially clavichord music, for the clavichord was the cantabile instrument *par excellence*. Keyboard music described merely as 'a 2 Clav. e Ped.' (e.g. Bach's keyboard trio-sonatas) is usually not for the organ nor yet for the pedal-harpsichord; as Susi Jeans pointed out some time ago, music of this kind was primarily designed for the organist's favourite

c*

practice instrument, a pedal-clavichord. This consisted of two clavichords mounted one above the other, with a pedal keyboard underneath.

French and English music is usually for the harpsichord. The French described the clavichord contemptuously as a mere 'box of flies', and it is difficult to find any evidence of its use in eighteenth-century France; the English, too, seemed to have used it very rarely indeed, and it is never mentioned on English title-pages. The words 'clavecin', 'clavicembalo' and 'harpsichord' have unambiguous meanings throughout the eighteenth century; they are exact synonyms, and they always refer to a plucked-string keyboard instrument. 'Cembalo' and 'Clavier' are used somewhat more loosely.

Italian music is usually for the harpsichord; but certain of Scarlatti's sonatas seem to have some of the special features listed in the table on page 73 as characteristic of clavichord or piano music, and these will sound at their best when played on a clavichord or piano.

Music with a thin texture (e.g. a treble melody accompanied by a rather distant bass-line) sounds so much better on the clavichord than it does on the harpsichord that it may be classed as clavichord music. Many of the pieces in Bach's Anna Magdalena Book fall into this category.

Music of the concerto grosso type (e.g. Bach's Italian Concerto, and the overtures—and consequently the remainder —of the English Suites) is for the harpsichord. Anything that requires the use of two manuals without a pedal (e.g. the Goldberg Variations) will be for harpsichord.

The '48' contain such a mixture of styles that it is impossible to state categorically which instrument they should be played on as a whole. Certain of them sound at their best on the harpsichord, others on the clavichord, and some on the organ. (To quote Avison: '[The Organ best expresses] the grand or solemn Stile, [the harpsichord] those lively or trickling Movements which thrill in the Ear.') At the end of the eighteenth century the word 'Clavier' acquired the fairly limited connotation of 'clavichord' or 'fortepiano', but its meaning at the beginning of the century was far less limited.

Fugues set out in full score, with no indication of instrumentation (e.g. Frescobaldi's ricercars, d'Anglebert's fugues, The Art of Fugue) are for the keyboard, not for an instrumental ensemble. They will probably sound best on the harpsichord or organ.

Lavish use of mordents, slides, trills and turns tends to be a characteristic of harpsichord music rather than of music for the clavichord or fortepiano. As C. P. E. Bach well knew, ornaments must be used much more precisely on the clavichord and fortepiano than on the harpsichord. The mechanism of the harpsichord and organ ensures that the main note of an ornament is exactly as loud as its auxiliaries, and this absolute equality gives these ornaments a snap and glitter which they can never have on the less rigid mechanism of the clavichord or piano. When early music is played on the piano, therefore, the whole question of ornaments needs considering with the greatest care. In much eighteenth-century music the ornaments are an integral part of the texture; Couperin (1722), for instance, writes emphatically on this point:

> I am always painfully surprised (after all the care I have taken to mark all the appropriate ornaments in my music . . .) to hear my pieces played by people who have learned them without taking the trouble to follow my directions. This negligence is unpardonable, for the choice of ornaments is no mere question of personal preference. I therefore declare that my pieces ought to be played exactly as I have marked them, with no additions or omissions; for otherwise they will never make their proper impression on persons of good taste.

Pianists who eliminate every ornament fly in the face of the clearly expressed views of Couperin and his contemporaries.

A certain amount of seventeenth- and early eighteenth-century music has survived in manuscripts written in an old-fashioned kind of notation usually known as German organ tablature. Broadly speaking it is true to say that the only people who knew how to read this notation were organists, and we must conclude therefore that music of this kind was associated with the instruments that organists were especially familiar with—the organ and the clavichord. Perhaps the most important document of this kind is the large volume of hitherto unknown music (dance-suites and variations) by Buxtehude, discovered in Denmark during the Second World War. The style of the music is ill-suited to the organ and its texture is not that of harpsichord music; but it is perfect clavichord music, and the evidence of its original notation suggests almost without a doubt that this was the instrument for which it was intended.

The stylistic pointers outlined very briefly in the preceding paragraphs may help the player to discover the instrument for which any given piece of early keyboard music was in all probability originally written. But it would be absurdly impertinent and visionary to suggest that present-day performances of this music should be confined entirely to those given on the original instruments. For one thing, few people have the time, money and knowledge that are needed to become a clavichordist or harpsichordist, as distinct from a clavichord- or harpsichord-player. A bad player can make either of these instruments sound very dismal indeed, and earlier ages were more sensitive than we have yet become to the shortcomings of bad players and to the beauties of good touch. A contemporary critic remarked of Chambonnières that:

> if he played a chord and another person played exactly the same chord immediately after him, there was always a great difference between the two versions; the reason for this was . . . that he had an approach and a style of setting his fingers to the keys that was unknown to other players;

and this is only one reference among many. But far more important than these nice points of touch and technique is the fact that early keyboard music is too universal in its appeal to be restricted to a narrow circle. This music has been regularly, widely and lovingly performed on the piano for more than a century, and anyone who tries to build a fence round it will be no more successful at cuckoo-catching than were the Three Wise Men of Gotham. All the enthusiast has any right to ask is that the keyboard-player, no matter what his instrument, should do all he can to meet an early composer on his own ground by discovering the lines along which he thought and the way in which he planned and played his music; for there is no other way of bridging the broken years between 'then' and 'now'. And at the same time every player ought to keep in mind Avison's remark:

> One of the best general Rules, perhaps, that can be given for Musical Expression, is that which gives rise to the Pathetic in every other Art, *an unaffected Strain of Nature and Simplicity*.

THE THREE STYLES

For a great part of the eighteenth century two distinct national styles of composition and performance, the French and the Italian, were in international use. Even at the beginning of the century the dividing lines between the styles are not always as clearly defined as the tidy-minded scholar might wish, and the styles coalesced in the middle years of the century into the third style, the *galant*. In addition to these, a distinctive German style was in use in Germany during the early years of the eighteenth century; this is seen at its clearest in some of Bach's organ preludes and fugues and chorale-preludes, and in the partitas of his predecessors (e.g. Georg Böhm) and contemporaries. This style presents few problems to the student of interpretation, for there are no special idiosyncrasies of notation or performance especially associated with it.

But there are very definite idiosyncrasies of this kind connected with the other three styles, and the performer ought therefore to be able to distinguish between them. Composers like Bach or Telemann were perfectly capable of writing music for church, stage or chamber in any or all of the styles, and they expected the performer to be able to appreciate which of them was being used in any particular piece. Avison (1752) has some valuable remarks to make on this point, as on so many others:

> The different species of Music for the *Church*, the *Theatre*, or the *Chamber*, are, or should be, distinguished by their peculiar Expression. [A footnote quotes, from Tosi: By the *Ancients*, *Airs* were sung in three different Manners; for the Theatre, the Style

was lively and various; for the Chamber, delicate and finished; for the Church, moving and grave. This Difference, to very many Moderns, is quite unknown.] . . . For Instance, the Words *Andante*, *Presto*, *Allegro*, etc. are differently apply'd in the different Kinds of Music above-mentioned. . . .

There are but three Circumstances on which the worth of any musical Composition can depend. These are *Melody*, *Harmony*, and *Expression*. When these are united in their full Excellence, the Composition is then perfect: If any of these are wanting or imperfect, the Composition is proportionably defective. . . .

We may, perhaps, affirm with Truth, that *Inequality* makes a Part of the Character of Excellence: That something ought to be thrown into Shades, in order to make the Lights more striking. . . .

As *Musical Expression* in the *Composer*, is succeeding in the Attempt to express some particular Passion; so in the *Performer*, it is to do a *Composition* Justice, by playing it in a *Taste* and *Stile* so exactly corresponding with the Intention of the Composer, as to preserve and illustrate *all* the Beauties of his Work.

THE FRENCH STYLE

Broadly speaking, this was based on the characteristic features of French music written between 1650 and 1700 by Lully, his contemporaries and their successors. It remained in fashion in France until at least the middle of the eighteenth century. The notational problems it presents are substantial, and the style of performance with which they were associated was very mannered.[1] Neither notation nor performance in this style can be comprehensively discussed in a book of this size, and the interested reader must go to the original sources and follow up the matter for himself. Many of these sources are to be found in translation in the treatises of Dannreuther

[1] Perhaps the best present-day examples of mannered performance may be found in jazz music. The deliberate stylizations associated with it are innumerable: special vowel sounds, the use of just intonation in vocal close harmony, 'blue' notes, polychoral writing for brass, continuo-playing in the guitars and rhythm section, a preference for unequal quavers in conjunct motion, exaggeratedly dotted rhythms, ornaments of every kind, and 'gimmicks' ranging from synthetic echo effects to the use of multiple sound-tracks. The student of the history of performance will find much to interest him here; many of these devices are debased or improved versions of the mannered styles used in 'classical' music at various stages of its development.

and Dolmetsch; but these pioneering writers did not always critically assess or correctly use the information they derived from their sources. Neglect of the essential features inherent in the French style will lead to a totally false conception of how music written in this style should be performed. Perhaps the clearest account of it is to be found in Couperin's harpsichord tutor (1716–17), and what he has to say about harpsichord-playing applies to most of the French music of his time and to the French style in general. His book has been chosen as the basis for this discussion in preference to the similar treatises for viol and flute written by his contemporaries, for Couperin is a well-known composer and they are not; Couperin's remarks are exactly paralleled by those of men like Hotteterre, Rousseau and Marais, and his name commands greater respect than theirs. Moreover he goes into the subject in great detail; for, as he rather ingenuously says, 'everyone in Paris wants to play in an up-to-date way; Paris is the centre of good taste, and I am a Parisian; since my book is the first of its kind and may well have a wide circulation, I have therefore omitted nothing'. His remarks are summarized in the next paragraphs, and they have been supplemented here and there from the writings of Marais (1692), Loulié (1696), St Lambert (1702), Hotteterre (1728), Quantz (1752) and Dom Bédos de Celles (1766).

'In this book,' he says, 'I shall treat of everything that has to do with good harpsichord-playing, and I trust that my notions of the style proper to this instrument will be set out sufficiently clearly to help those who want to become skilful and to be approved of by those players who are already expert. Though the distance between Grammar and Rhetoric is great enough, the distance between musical notation and the art of playing well is infinitely greater. I need not fear that enlightened performers will misunderstand me, but I must urge the others to be docile and to lay aside any prejudices they may have. And in any case I assure everyone that these rules of mine are absolutely vital to anyone who wants to succeed in playing my music properly.'

(Couperin then goes on to discuss certain immensely important points of harpsichord technique, most of which are too specialized to be reproduced here. The following remarks are of wider importance, however.) 'It has hitherto appeared almost impossible to maintain that the harpsichord can be made to sound expressive, but this can be done by means of the *aspiration* and the *suspension*. The *suspension*—a note played late—corresponds to a crescendo on a stringed instrument, and is scarcely used except in slow and tender pieces. The *aspiration*—a note quitted early—corresponds to a diminuendo, and it should be less abrupt in a slow piece than in a quick one. The long mordent on the harpsichord corresponds to a vibrato on a bowed instrument. Appoggiaturas of every kind must be struck on the beat, not before it ("you dwell longer on the Preparation than on the Note for which the Preparation is made": J. E. Galliard, 1724). But the *coulé*, used mostly for filling in the gaps in a chain of descending thirds, is played before the beat and slurred on to the note which follows it. Shakes must always begin on the upper note, and they must grow faster towards the end, though the gradation of speed ought to be imperceptible; do not begin them too soon. Slow pieces should be played a little faster on the harpsichord than they would be on other instruments. Preludes should be played freely and with plenty of rubato, except when the word *mesuré* occurs; in this case they are to be played in strict time. The difference between these two styles is rather like the distinction between poetry and prose. . . .

'It seems to me that there are errors in the notation we use in France which are rather like the errors in the spelling of the French language. What we see does not correspond to what we hear, and in consequence foreigners do not play our music as well as we play theirs. Italian music, for instance, tends to be abstract, ours—whether for violin, viol or harpsichord— tries to express some definite mood, indicated by means of a word like *tendrement* or *vivement*; a good pupil can be judged by his ability to realize at once the proper mood of any piece of music. The Italians write their music in its true time-values, but we do not. They play a diatonic succession of quavers evenly, whereas we always make the first of each pair a little longer than the second. This inequality should be more pronounced in a gay piece than in a sad one; but there are certain places where it must not be used. One is shown by a slur over each pair, the second note being dotted; this means that the second note must be longer than the first.[1] Another occurs when every note is dotted; this does not mean that the notes are to be played staccato but that they are to be played perfectly evenly. And rapid music (allemandes, for instance); repeated or disjunct notes; equal notes in any music other than French; notes slurred together more than two at a time; and notes mixed with shorter notes: these must all be played equally. The words *notes égalles* or *mesuré* are used to denote the same thing.'

Rhythms that are already written as dotted ones, whether they are iambic or trochaic, need to have the disparity between the lengths of the notes emphasized; otherwise they will sound lazy. (One important exception to this is given by Quantz, which applies to the D major fugue of the '48', book I; if 𝅘𝅥𝅯𝅘𝅥𝅯𝅘𝅥𝅯 and 𝅘𝅥𝅮𝅘𝅥𝅯 occur side by side or simultaneously, the dotted rhythm is played as it is written.) A short rest before the shorter note will improve the articulation; rests of this kind will be found in the first movement of Bach's keyboard partita in B minor. But neither Bach nor his contemporaries usually bothered to write them out in full, nor to indicate the exact length of short notes in pieces that make use of dotted rhythms; as a result these pieces are scarcely ever performed correctly at the present day. In an overture in the French style (HAM 223–4), for instance, all the parts should move together, jerkily, even when their written note-values do not suggest that this is how they should be played. *All* dotted rhythms should be adjusted so that they fit the shortest one in the piece; this will often mean that the first note after a rest will need shortening, ¢ 𝄾 𝅘𝅥𝅮𝅘𝅥𝅮.𝅘𝅥𝅯𝅘𝅥𝅮. 𝅘𝅥𝅮 becoming ¢ 𝄾𝄾.𝅘𝅥𝅮𝅘𝅥𝅮.𝅘𝅥𝅯𝅘𝅥𝅮. 𝅘𝅥𝅯 in performance. Alterations of the written rhythms will be commonest in pieces written in 2, ¢, 3/4 and 6/4.

This conventional lengthening of the dotted note and shortening of the complementary note was in very widespread use over a very great length of time, and ignorance of this fact is one of the gravest defects of present-day performances

[1]See musical example on p. 12.

of old music. It is a fashion that lasted from the early years of the seventeenth century down to the last years of the nineteenth, and it still survives in the march-playing of a good military band, though it has become obsolete among orchestral players and pianists. It is required in Monteverdi and Purcell (see Chapter VI); in the overtures to Handel's oratorios and operas; in the overtures to Bach's orchestral suites and to such works as the harpsichord Partita in C minor. It applies to marches and to sicilianos, to jigs and to Andantes. Quantz and C. P. E. Bach are unanimous in saying that it applies to the music of their own time. It is found in some of Gluck's operas, as well as in those of Sarti. Leopold Mozart (1756) prescribes it for Adagios or in any piece that would otherwise sound lazy. It is implied in Haydn, Mozart and Beethoven; though these men wrote no books on the interpretation of their music, their pieces for mechanical clock show that they expected this convention to be applied to the notation they used. Evidence from these clocks is of the highest value, for the pieces they play have often survived in the double form of manuscript copies and of pins set in a metal barrel. Now a clock cannot be taught to play stylishly; its mechanism must therefore provide it with the exact duration of any note. Consequently these clocks, like gramophone discs, provide exact and lasting evidence of how certain written rhythms were performed at the time the barrels were made.

No. 27 of the modern edition of Haydn's clock-pieces is a Siciliano in 6/8 time. The written rhythm is $\frac{6}{8}$ ♪ | ♫ ♫ | ♫ ♫ | but the pinning of the barrel shows that this should be performed as $\frac{6}{8}$ ♪ | ♫ ♫ | ♫ ♫ |. The tradition can in the same way be shown to apply to Mozart and Beethoven; thus the dotted rhythms in Mozart's wonderful Rondo in A minor (K. 511) and in the *Marcia alla francese* from his Divertimento in D major (K. 251) are not to be played as they are written. For Beethoven's time it is confirmed by sources as diverse as an English flute-tutor of 1794 and Koch's *Lexicon* (1802), and though the double dot was then coming into increasing use there is every reason to suppose that Beethoven and his contemporaries did not use it nearly as systematically as we do today. It may at first seem rather surprising that composers continued to use this inexact notation for so long; but it was very much quicker and less fussy to write, and its correct performance was the sort of thing that is far easier to explain at a rehearsal than to write out in full. This can be easily confirmed by anyone who likes to try it.

So much for the rhythmic problems of the French style and of the styles deriving from it. Most of the other interpretative mannerisms associated with it are to be deduced not from Couperin and the other sources used for the preceding paragraphs but from documents like the prefaces to Cousser's orchestral suites (1682) and those of Georg Muffat (1695–8), Raguenet's *Comparison between French and Italian Music* (1702: English translation, 1709), and de Freneuse's essay on the same subject (1704–5). Muffat's suites, like those of so many of his German and Austrian contemporaries (including those of Bach), were deliberately written in the French style, modelled on the operatic overtures and dances of Lully. Since Muffat's were amongst the first composed by any composer not of French birth, Muffat was careful to explain in some detail (and in no fewer than four languages) exactly how novel they were and exactly how they were to be played in accordance with the French style. The following paragraphs summarize the evidence provided by these and other sources of the time.

(1) Tempo: C is to be beaten in 4; ₵ and 2 are twice as fast. *Overtures*, *préludes* and *symphonies* in 2 are fairly slow, *ballets* in 2 somewhat faster. *Gavottes* in ₵ are slower than *bourrées* in C. The quaver in 2 is about as fast as the quaver in an Italian *presto* in C; but in the French style successive conjunct quavers are to be played unevenly, in contrast to the even rhythms of Italian music. 3/2 is fairly slow, 3/4 in a *sarabande* or *air* somewhat faster. A *rondeau* in 3/4 is lively and a *courante, fugue* or *menuet* in 3/4 very brisk (compare Brossard [1703]: 'Menuet—very gay and very fast; properly speaking it should be written in 3/8 or 6/8, in imitation of the Italians'). *Gigues* and *canaries* are to be played the fastest of all, no matter what their time-signature.

These remarks on time-signatures and tempo may be

compared with the evidence provided by Purcell's book of
harpsichord pieces (1696) and the attempts at chronometric
tempi made by Michel L'Affilard (1694). L'Affilard's tempi
are here expressed in terms of modern metronome marks.

	Purcell	L'Affilard
C	slow	
¢	a little faster	marche: crotchet=95
₡	brisk and airy	—
2	—	gavotte, rigaudon, etc.: minim=120
3/4	slow	sarabande en rondeau: crotchet=86
		passacaille: crotchet= 106
3	faster	chaconne: crotchet=156
		menuet: dotted minim=70
3/2	very slow	sarabande: minim=72
	(except hornpipe)	courante: minim=90
3/8	—	passepied: dotted crotchet=86
		gigue: dotted crotchet= 116
6/4	brisk	sarabande: crotchet=133
		marche: crotchet=150
6/8	—	canaries: dotted crotchet=106
		gigue: dotted crotchet=100

(2) Bowing: Players should play uniformly, with a full
tone in tuttis and a soft tender tone in solos. All notes are to be
bowed separately, except where otherwise marked, and Lully's
rule that there should be a down-bow on every strong beat
should be carefully observed. It may be broken, if necessary,
in very fast pieces. The tone should never be forced, and the
music must always be soft, flowing, singing, easy and coherent.
'The three things required of a player are exactness, delicacy,
and getting the most out of his instrument.' The inner parts
of the texture are comparatively unimportant and should
never be over-emphasized (Lully is reputed to have written
much of his music as a skeleton for treble and figured bass,
leaving his pupils and assistants to fill in the inner parts;
these are seldom very distinguished, and the story may well
be true). Keep to the first three left-hand positions for preference, and by all means use a little vibrato; but let this be
fairly slow and adapted to the expression of the piece as a

whole. Couperin's rules for fingering the harpsichord will provide valuable evidence for the French taste in phrasing; both he and Rameau use slurs with great precision, and both are careful to group their notes in order to show the correct phrasing. Couperin's use of the comma is very eloquent. In the preface to Book III of his harpsichord pieces he explains that this is used to mark the end of melodic or harmonic phrases, and denotes the slightest of breaks, which must never be allowed to distort the rhythm. (Examples of its use are in HAM 265.)

(3) Ornaments: These in ensemble music are commonly indicated by a single sign (+), or even omitted altogether. The sign should be interpreted to mean an appoggiatura, a trill, a mordent or any other appropriate ornament according to their context. Mondonville's sonatas for violin and harpsichord (1734) will be useful here, for the harpsichord part has the proper signs for ornaments where the violin part has only crosses. Muffat's suggestions for them may be summarized thus: (i) inverted mordents for showing stress; (ii) trills only when they can be played as diatonic semitones, and never on opening notes nor (usually) on notes approached by a leap; they may be used more liberally in descending scale passages, especially on dotted notes; (iii) appoggiaturas on notes approached by a leap from below and (with or without a mordent) on strong beats in rising scale passages; (iv) *coulements* on notes approached by a leap from below; (v) rapid scales to show vehemence; their French name is *tirades*, and like tirades they should be rare; (vi) *coulés* in falling intervals and leaps down, with a trill on the last note. Ornaments must be tender, well-chosen, not too frequent nor too fast, yet animated. A few bars from HAM 224, edited in accordance with the French style of performance, will be found on p. 169.

Muffat's remark:

Those who condemn the ornaments of the French style out of hand because they stifle the tune or the harmony have never heard Lully's true pupils but only his false imitators.

may be contrasted with Burney's :

[Couperin's] pieces are so crowded and deformed by beats, trills and shakes, that no plain note was ever left to enable the hearer of them to judge whether the tone of the instrument on which they were played was good or bad.

Burney's often ill-considered judgements are at the root of only too much nineteenth- and twentieth-century thought about old music, and it is time that we outgrew them.

THE ITALIAN STYLE

The objections raised by the seventeenth- and early eighteenth-century Frenchman to the Italian style are those that his nineteenth-century compatriots raised against Wagner: that it was too noisy and too complicated. De Marolles makes this point as early as 1657, and de Freneuse congratulates the French violinist, Rebel, on the way in which he has tempered the Italian style to the French taste.

The Italian style is less sophisticated, less mannered, and less subtle and restrained than the French style. It presents far fewer problems to the performer of our own time chiefly because the notation used by Italian composers almost always means what it says, and so needs no pulling about. The two great exceptions to this rule are the gracing of an Adagio, and the treatment of dotted rhythms. In the typical Italian Adagio of the eighteenth century the player was expected to improvise fairly freely on the melody in front of him; the composer's notes were a mere skeleton, to be clothed in runs, roulades, ornaments and embroidery of every kind. Thus in the whole of Corelli's published output only one slow movement (Op. VI, no. 8) is directed to be played 'sostenuto and as it stands'; all the others were intended to be liberally graced by the performer.

In Italy this traditional technique was a very old one. It required a thorough knowledge of harmony and counterpoint on the part of the player, and it can be traced back at least to the early years of the sixteenth century. A manuscript of that date now in the town library at Trent shows how a viol-player was expected to be able to improvise a free part of his own to two parts taken from a well-known chanson and played on a keyboard instrument. The same technique is found in Diego Ortiz's treatise on viol-playing (1553); a player is there taught how to extemporize a fifth part to a four-part madrigal or chanson, and how to transform any one of the given parts into a most brilliant solo for the viol by the addition of ornaments and roulades. Dalla Casa's book on divisions (1584) teaches the same technique; in addition he deals with a new one, characteristic of the lyra bastarda, in which all four parts of a madrigal are reduced to a single extemporized part whose filigree of notes and runs sketches the harmony and counterpoint of the whole polyphonic original. This Italian technique, introduced into England by men like the younger Ferrabosco and Angelo Notari, led to the division-viol music of the seventeenth century, but it was not forgotten in the land of its origin. The slow movements of some of the trio-sonatas of M. A. Ferro (1649) are intended to be extemporized by the gambist and the violinist in alternation, over a ground bass played by the harpsichord. From Ferro to Torelli and Corelli is but a short step, and there was no break in the tradition that stretched from the Trent manuscript to the violin sonatas of the great Italian composers of the early eighteenth century.

Many examples of how this gracing of a slow movement was done are still in existence. Corelli's solo sonatas (Op. V) were first published in Rome in 1700, but pirated editions were soon made by the two rival publishing houses of Amsterdam, Roger and Mortier. Roger, who knew a great deal about salesmanship as well as about music, advertised his edition as 'engraved . . . with graces for the Adagios as M. Corelli wants them to be played; and anyone who wants to see M. Corelli's original, and his letters dealing with the subject, has only to ask at my shop'. This edition in its turn was pirated by Walsh of London, and the sonatas remained in favour among English music-lovers for nearly a century and a half after they were first published. In the preface to his edition of them in score (1839), Czerny says:

Corelli's 12 Solos have for many years been considered as an extremely important and useful practical work. . . . It is therefore

to be presumed, that a newly revised, and carefully corrected
Edition . . . cannot but prove highly acceptable to every Learner
of the Pianoforte, the Harp, the Violin, the Violoncello, and
Thorough Bass. . . . In undertaking this new revision and en-
largement of this truly Classical production of CORELLI, the
undersigned believes that he has contributed an important
assistance to the advancement of youthful Talent; and one which
he hopes will not be deemed unworthy of general approbation.

His edition was still in print up to a year or two ago, but for
the present inquiry it is of less value than the edition made
by Joachim and Chrysander in 1891, for this reproduces the
embellishments of the Roger-Mortier-Walsh edition; these
are thus easily accessible to the interested player of the present
day (see also HAM 252).

But these were by no means the only embellished versions
of the works current at the time. Hawkins's *History* (pp. 904–7
of the edition of 1875) prints a sonata as it was played by
Geminiani; a manuscript in M. Cortot's library contains
'Correlli's Solos, graced by Doburg' (i.e. Matthew Dubourg,
who played for the Dublin performances of Messiah in 1742:
it is said that he once set out on such a long and elaborate
cadenza that when he finally reached its end Handel's voice
greeted him with 'Welcome home, Mr Dubourg'). In this
manuscript nearly every movement is ornamented in the most
extravagant way. While some of Dubourg's ornamentation
lends sparkle to what would otherwise be a rather insipid
repeat, the general impression it leaves is one of overwhelming
conceit and lack of taste. The Adagios are the best and most
eloquent examples of his special skill. But it must be emphasized once again that these examples of graced slow movements are to be taken as models for extemporization, not as
texts to be learned and then played note-for-note in an actual
present-day performance. The lost art of extemporization is
as essential for this as it is for continuo-playing.

It has already been pointed out that in the Italian style
music is generally written as it is played, with the exception of
Adagios. But there are certain idiosyncrasies in the notation of
dotted rhythms which may mislead the ingenuous player.
Trochaic and anapaestic rhythms occurring in a march, a

siciliano or a grave should usually be performed somewhat more dottedly than they are written; in this respect the French and the Italian styles agree. A more intricate problem is presented by trochaic rhythms in compound triple time; these are often written as dotted rhythms when in fact they should be performed in conformity with the dominant triplet rhythm of the movement. For instance, rhythms intended to sound as

will often be written as

(Handel) (Corelli) (Bach)

But the proper treatment of the original notation of these examples as of so many others can be summed up in a single phrase: *assimilate all dotted rhythms to the dominant rhythm of the movement.* As a rule-of-thumb method this will usually work pretty well; it works throughout the gigue of HAM 253, for instance, in the bass part (the pairs of equal quavers in the continuo part should all be made trochaic).

In the Italian style, then, departures from the written text fall into the following categories: extemporized embellishment of Adagios; optional variation of repeated material; additional ornamentation at cadences, varying from a trill to a whole cadenza; slight alterations of written note-values always associated with the occurrence of trochaic, anapaestic or triplet rhythms elsewhere in the same movement (the whole of HAM 283 should be played as though it were written as a march in 6/4).

As far as the Italian style of playing is concerned, much can be deduced from the essays of Raguenet and his French contemporaries (e.g. the 'Dissertation sur la musique italienne et françoise de M. de L.T.' printed in the *Mercure de France*, November 1713), and the prefaces to such collections as Muffat's concertos in the Italian style (1701). This may be amplified very considerably by reference to Geminiani's treatises and other contemporary books of the same kind, many of them published in England. In general, the Italian style is more fiery and impetuous; the instrumental music is more violinistic, the vocal music more operatic, than the French music of the same period (see, for instance, HAM 259, 260, 263, 269, 270, 275). Woodwind instruments were far less used in Italy than they were in France, as Raguenet points out:

> Besides all the instruments that are common to [the French] as well as the Italians, [the French] have the Hautboys, which by their sounds, equally mellow and piercing, have infinitely the advantage of the violins in all brisk, lively airs, and the flutes, which so many of our great artists have taught to groan after so moving a manner in our moanful airs, and sigh so amorously in those that are tender.

Raguenet's remarks may be compared with those of Avison and his teacher, Geminiani:

> The *Hautboy* will best express the *Cantabile*, or singing Style, and may be used in all Movements whatever under this Denomination; especially those movements which tend to the *Gay* and *Chearful.* . . . The *German* flute . . . will best express the languishing, or melancholy Style. . . . With both these Instruments, the running into *extreme* Keys, the Use of the *Staccato*, or distinct Separation of Notes, and all irregular Leaps, or broken and uneven Intervals must be avoided.
>
> Avison (1752)

> I must not however omit to observe that the excellence of [the flute] consists in the *Cantabile*, as that gives Time to regulate the Breath, and not in swift Movements where there are *Arpeggios* and *Jumping Notes*. Indeed those who study with an Intent to please should know the *Fort* and the *Feeble* of their Instrument, in order to avoid the Error of him, who laboured for a long While to be able to Sing, Play and Dance three different Airs at once: and being presented to Lewis XIV for a wonderful Person, that Monarch after having seen his Performance, said, *what this Man does may be very difficult, but is not pleasing.*
>
> Geminiani (*c.* 1745)

And though in his next paragraphs Raguenet is chiefly concerned with the Italian style of singing, everything he says is true of the Italian style of performance in general; to quote Avison (1752):

> As the finest *instrumental Music* may be considered as an Imitation of the *vocal*; so do [the string] Instruments, with their expressive Tone and the minutest Changes they are capable of in the Progression of Melody, shew their nearest Approaches to the Perfection of the human Voice.

Raguenet continues:

> [The French] flatter, tickle, and court the ear and are still doubtful of success, though everything be done with an exact regularity. . . . The Italians venture at everything that is harsh and out of the way, but then they do it like people that have a right to venture and are sure of success. . . . They are more sensible of the passions and consequently express 'em more lively in all their productions. If a storm or rage is to be described in a symphony, their notes give us so natural an idea of it that our souls can hardly receive a stronger impression from the reality than they do from the description. . . . The artist himself whilst he is performing it, is seized with an unavoidable agony; he tortures his violin; he racks his body; [here a footnote describes Corelli's playing in similar terms]. . . . If, on the other side, the symphony is to express a calm and tranquility, which requires a quite different style, they however execute it with an equal success. . . . Every string of the bow is of an infinite length, lingering on a dying sound which decays gradually till at last it absolutely expires. . . .
>
> Their violins are mounted with strings much larger than ours; their bows are longer, and they can make their instruments sound as loud again as ours. . . . Their archlutes are as large again as our theorbos and their sound consequently louder by half; their [cellos] are as large again as the French [bass-viols], and all ours put together don't sound so loud in our operas as two or three of those basses in Italy.

Geminiani (1751) goes into greater technical detail; and only a précis of his remarks can be given here. 'The best performers are least sparing of their Bows'; but strong beats must not be stressed in a dull or mechanical way (compare the French style, in which this metrical accentuation is an essential feature of the performance). Slow notes must be reasonably legato, with a *messa di voce*; rapid semiquavers 'are to be play'd plain and the Bow is not to be taken off the Strings', though a detached bow-stroke is good for rapid crotchets and quavers. Avison (1752) does not hold with double stops:

> Even the Use of double Stops on [the violin] may, in my Opinion, be considered as one of the Abuses of it; since, in the Hands of the greatest Masters, they only deaden the tone, spoil the Expression, and obstruct the Execution. In a Word, they baffle the Performer's Art, and bring down *one good* Instrument to the State of *two indifferent ones*.

Muffat (1701) adds a few more details. The first note of the piece and any note entering after a rest is to be played boldly and loudly by the whole band. Pianos and fortes are to be strongly contrasted, and so are Adagios and Prestos. There must be no slackening of the tone in suspensions and their resolutions, the movement of the individual parts being accentuated by a slight articulation rather than weakened by a timid slur. Final notes must be held to their full value and all repetitions must be played—indeed lively movements may be played three times, if you like. But never repeat a Grave. Two, much less three, concertos or sonatas of the same kind should never be played in succession, for the listener's attention will wander.

Martinelli (1768) states that Corelli's aim was always to preserve a natural and singing tone; hence what appears at first to be his rather unenterprising preference for the middle register. A famous anecdote about Corelli shows how clear-cut was the division between the French and the Italian styles at the time when Handel was in Italy as a young man (1706–10). It seems that Corelli was leading the overture of *Il Trionfo di Tempo*, with Handel playing the continuo. Corelli played listlessly and without fire; eventually Handel could bear it no longer and, leaping from his seat, he snatched Corelli's violin out of his hands in order to show him the correct way in which the piece should be played. The gentle Corelli was not at all put out, and excused himself by saying: 'But, my dear Saxon, this music is in the French style, which I do not understand.'

A final quotation from Avison (1752) provides us with some valuable information about the constitution of an 'Italian' orchestra, and the way in which a concerto grosso should be played. The group of soloists should be matched by a ripieno section consisting of six first violins, four seconds, four cellos, two double basses and a harpsichord; ripieno violas were not used in the type of concerto with which Avison was chiefly concerned, but if they had been Avison would probably have suggested that three of them be included in an orchestra of this size.

> A lesser Number of Instruments, near the same Proportion, will also have a proper Effect, and may answer the Composer's Intention; but more would probably destroy the just Contrast, which should always be kept up between the Chorus and Solo. . . .
> The Use of the *Acciaccatura*, or Sweeping of the Chords, and the dropping or sprinkling Notes, are indeed one of the peculiar Beauties of [the harpsichord]. But these graceful Touches are only reserved for a Masterly Application in the Accompanyment of a fine Voice, or single Instrument; and therefore . . . they are not required in the Performance of full Music.

THE DIFFUSION OF THE STYLES

The contrast between the French and the Italian styles can be seen at its clearest, perhaps, in works like Couperin's 'L'Apothéose de Corelli' (1722) and 'L'Apothéose de Lully' (1725). In works like Batistin's 'L'Union de la musique fran-çaise et de la musique italienne' or Aubert's 'Concerts de symphonie' (1730) the composers definitely set out to fuse the two styles into one. But their example, which was to lean towards the galant style of the middle years of the century, was little followed outside a small circle of Parisian musicians and composers, and most music continued to be deliberately written in one style or the other. Couperin's early sonatas (1692–5) are Italian; the suites he added to them in 1724 are

French, like his 'Concerts royaux' of the same period. Fux's 'Concentus Musico-instrumentalis' (1701) is Italian for the most part, though it contains one interesting sonata directly contrasting the two styles. Böhm's keyboard suites are heavily influenced by the French style; his table of ornaments is reproduced in its entirety from Dieupart's. Dandrieu wrote violin sonatas containing nothing but movements in the Italian style (Adagio—Allemanda—Siciliana—Gavotta—Vivace); yet his keyboard suites are completely French. In the preface to his concertos of 1701, Muffat emphasizes the contrast between the two styles by bowing the same passage first in the French and then in the Italian style (this is reproduced on p. 171). Loeillet's keyboard suites (c. 1710) contain movements in both styles; so do those by Boutmy (1738 and 1750) and Fiocco (c. 1730). J. K. F. Fischer's suites are clearly French. Telemann, even more eclectic than Bach in his musical tastes, wrote much music in the French style; he also composed sets of pieces designed to display each of the styles in turn (e.g. his thirty-six keyboard fantasies). And both Bach and Handel are known to have transcribed and studied French and Italian music in order to gain a closer acquaintance with the features that distinguished the one style from the other.

How then may the two styles be most easily recognized? What are the most obvious clues in any piece? The answer is: its title, and certain features of its texture and instrumentation. Suites are French, sonatas and concertos are Italian. Dances with titles spelled in the French way (allemande, courante, gigue, bourrée, sarabande, and so on) and French tempo-indications (vivement, lentement) call for a French style of performance; dances with Italian titles (allemanda, corrente, siciliano, giga, sarabanda) or Italian tempo-indications (allegro, grave, presto, adagio) demand an Italian style. Overtures are French, sinfonias Italian; and these two types of overture are not only formally distinct but also require to be played in different ways. Undulating rhythms and orchestration using obbligato wind instruments usually point to the French style; regular 'sewing-machine' rhythms, Scotch snaps, and predominantly string orchestration are characteristic of the Italian style.

A survey of some of Bach's music may illustrate these features more clearly. *The English suites:* all the courantes, bourrées, gavottes and sarabandes (except the sarabande in Suite V, perhaps) are French; the allemandes, gigues (except in Suite VI) and preludes are Italian. *The French suites:* courantes I and III are French and the others are Italian correntes (this indeed is Bach's own spelling for these, though even the Bach-Gesellschaft edition irons out the distinction); gigues I and II are French, and the others are Italian; the sarabandes are a mixture of the two styles.[1] *The '48':* the fugues are mostly German (though I, 10, for instance, is Italian); the preludes tend to be in a rather indeterminate style in general, so that they do not need to be fussed over; but I, 2, 5, and 6, and II, 16 are Italian, I, 4 and perhaps 8 are French, and II, 7 and 12 are in the new *galant* style, as is the trio from the *Musical Offering*. *The four orchestral suites:* these are thoroughly French, and the overtures will need to be played in an exaggeratedly French manner with plenty of double-dotting; courantes must have the sinuous and hesitant rhythm of the French style; passepieds must be fast; the little notes at the beginning of the sarabande in Suite II are coulés, not appoggiaturas. But the air and gigue in Suite III are italianate, like the fugue in the overture to Suite IV; and all the minuets are called 'Menuetto', and are therefore to be played in the Italian manner and not too fast. *The concertos:* all these are Italian, and the slow movements of works like the Italian concerto or the keyboard concerto in F minor are magnificent examples of the gracing of an Adagio in the Italian manner; for further examples, see Bach's transcriptions for keyboard solo of sixteen concertos in the Italian style by Marcello, Telemann, Vivaldi and others.

The works for unaccompanied violin: Bach is careful to describe I, III and V as 'sonatas' and they are in the Italian style throughout; he described II, IV and VI as 'partitas' and they are for the most part Italian; in II, the 'courante' and 'sarabande' are Italian; the 'courante' in IV is also Italian and

---

[1]Sarabandes in 3/2 should always be slower than sarabandes in 3/4 during this period. This seems true for Bach and Handel, and it is demonstrably true for Corelli.

should therefore be played in a flowing 9/8 throughout, with none of the hesitations and subtleties of rhythm of a French courante; VI is stuffed with French dances, but the 'gigue' is Italian. *The works for unaccompanied cello:* in all except IV and V, the 'courantes' are Italian; the gigues in II and V are French, and so are the sarabandes in II and VI; but in general the style of these works is rather mixed, despite their French title of 'suites'. *The sonatas:* mostly Italian, but the player should watch for signs of the *galant* style, notably (as one might perhaps expect) in the flute sonatas.

THE GALANT STYLE

This has been mentioned once or twice in the preceding discussion but it has not yet been defined. The greatest contemporary authorities on the *galant* style are Quantz, C. P. E. Bach, Leopold Mozart and Marpurg; though the style may have been born in France, it was evidently raised in Germany. It is characterized by an extreme and rather finical sensibility in the treatment of ornaments, tempi and dynamics, and it is a synthetic style in which all the conflicting elements of the main styles of the early eighteenth century are fused into one; it points towards the 'classical' style of the later eighteenth century, yet the two styles are not identical. The strongest influence in *galant* music is probably Italian opera, and most of the characteristic features of its interpretation have to do with 'expression', in the widest sense of the word. *Galant* music must point, phrase by phrase, towards those sighing cadences which are so important a feature of the style; they are not mere clichés, but the emotional climaxes of the melodic line. The tune, its direction and its punctuation are all that matters. The gentler Allegros and Allegrettos must float, not scurry; the Graves and Adagios must be urbanely yet unashamedly emotional; and the finales must run, not scramble in a suffocating rush for the exit.

A few examples of the style can be found in Bach; the whole of the *Musical Offering* was written for a court in which *galant* taste in music was at its height, and though the fugues and canons are necessarily written in a learned style, the trio for flute, violin and continuo is one of the most *galant* of all Bach's works. The flute obbligato in 'Aus Liebe will mein Heiland sterben' from the *St Matthew Passion* is composed in a style so like Quantz's own that it is tempting to assume Quantz played it when it was first performed, and certain sarabandes in the keyboard works which stand midway between the true sarabande and the elegant polonaises of W. F. Bach (HAM 288) are also in the *galant* manner. But in general it is true to say that Bach was not very much at home in this style on the rare occasions on which he deliberately adopted it; though it was prefigured in the theoretical writings and in some of the music of men like Mattheson and Telemann, it was at its height during the years 1740 to 1780—the generation of Bach's sons (HAM 282, 284).

The clearest notion of the contemporary style of performance of *galant* music is perhaps to be derived from an examination of the Adagio for flute and continuo printed in Quantz's book. The flute part is given in two versions; the first is completely plain, the second embellished in accordance with Quantz's views on stylish performance (see p. 169). Every gradation of dynamics and phrasing is exactly marked, and the conclusions that can be drawn from studying this piece are exactly paralleled by the more theoretical discussions of the same topics in Quantz, C. P. E. Bach, Leopold Mozart, and Marpurg. The dynamics are constantly changing, in a way that is completely opposed to the terraced dynamics in fashion during the earlier part of the century, and the range of dynamics is extravagantly large. The embellishments lack the long lines of those by Geminiani or Dubourg; the phrasing is far more varied than it had ever been before, ranging from isolated staccatos to groups of ten or a dozen notes slurred together, and it is lavishly added to an original text that contains none at all; principal notes are usually played loudly, subsidiary ones dropping to an immediate piano; appoggiaturas grow ever softer as they resolve to their parent note; coulés and double appoggiaturas, however, are played softly and quickly, with a delicate accent; any chromatic note is always played more strongly, with a diminuendo immediately afterwards;

D

the first note of the piece begins pianissimo, and the last note dies away to nothing. The final result is exactly comparable to the contemporary taste for rococo ornament; all is artificial, sentimental, and highly mannered. When the flute obbligato in the *St Matthew Passion* is played in this way it lends a new character to the whole aria, setting it in high contrast to its neighbours; this was undoubtedly Bach's intention, though it is seldom realized in present-day performances of the work.

Quantz also gives us valuable information on what he considers to be the correct tempi for the music of his own time; but the interpreter must remember that this information cannot in general be taken as applying to the music of the earlier part of the century (in particular, to the music of J. S. Bach). For this period some sort of balance must be struck between the opinions of Quantz and those of Muffat and L'Affilard (see p. 84). Here is a summary of the more important of Quantz's suggestions.

For Italian tempo-marks in C:

Presto, Allegro assai	minim=80
Allegro moderato, Vivace	,, =60
Allegretto	crotchet=80
Adagio cantabile	,, =40
Adagio assai	,, =20

In ¢ all these speeds are doubled.

For dance forms with French titles:

Gigue, canarie (in 3/8)	dotted crotchet=160
Passacaille, tambourin	crotchet=180
Chaconne, furie, menuet, bourrée, rigaudon	,, =160
Rondeau	,, =140
Gavotte	,, =120
Marche (in ¢), Musette, courante, entrée louré	,, = 80

These are tempi for dancing; they should be somewhat modified or abstract music.

SOME MISCELLANEOUS MATTERS

No details of the original notation must be overlooked, for many of them had some special significance. Slurs, for instance, are used in much early music with a wide variety of meanings, and though some of these meanings are still current, others have been long forgotten. Among these obsolete usages, the following ones seem important:

(1) In French and German keyboard music from Buxtehude to Haydn, slurs over broken chord figures have a very precise meaning; they imply more than a mere legato, for the notes beneath them are to be held through to the end of the slur. This convention, like so many of those in C. P. E. Bach's book, applies to the whole of his father's music; 'In both composition and keyboard-playing, I have never had any teacher but my father', he says. Thus the slurs in the last bar of the E minor fugue from Book I of the '48', or in the partita in B minor, imply this ultra-legato interpretation, and there are other instances of its use which the player can discover for himself. Couperin, who developed a special set of conventional signs for use in his keyboard music, uses little slanting lines between the notes to indicate the same thing. The application of this rule quite transforms the keyboard music of this period, giving it weight and sonority.

(2) In German and Italian keyboard music a scale passage on the white keys written in very short notes with a slur over them is to be played glissando. This convention is found in Scarlatti and also in Bach (e.g. in the first movement of the C major concerto for two harpsichords, at bar 122).

(3) In music for horns and trumpets a slur between two different notes usually implies that the instrument should be overblown—in the best coach-horn manner—so that the lower note leaps without a break to the upper one. An instance of this convention may be found in the second and third bars of the first Brandenburg concerto. These often sound diffuse and mushy because of the cross-rhythms between the horns' triplets and the strongly marked quavers and semiquavers of the rest of the orchestra. But, as Eric Halfpenny has pointed

out, the horn figures reproduce two well-known hunting calls; the first, consisting of the same note repeated several times in succession, was called a 'ton', and the second, a low note overblown to the fifth above, a 'taverne'. The combination of the two is a 'ton-taverne' or tantivy. Bach was careful to mark the slur needed for the overblown 'taverne', so that the eighteenth-century player could be left in no doubt as to the proper way in which the notes should be played; but the modern player will naturally interpret the slur as denoting merely a legato. The proper effect should be one of hunting-calls ringing through the orchestral texture, not of fuzzy and uncertain rhythms; in a modern performance the proper dynamics at this point should therefore be *f molto cresc.* for the horns (bells up, perhaps? Certainly hand-stopping should not be used) and *mf* for the rest of the orchestra.

(4) Pairs of slurred quavers in Couperin, Rameau and other French writers, or in music in the French style, should be played according to the French interpretation of them (this will usually imply the inequality of rhythm dealt with on pp. 80–82). Slurs in Italian violin music are just as eloquent, and even if additional bowings are added in a modern performance they should not be allowed to obscure the distinction between slurred and unslurred notes that the composer has been at pains to indicate. This is a point to watch in the performance of Purcell's Italianate violin music, for instance: Purcell has marked slurred notes with great care, yet except for the volumes devoted to them in his complete works, there is scarcely one present-day edition of the trio-sonatas in which the composer's precise indications have been respected. The same is true of his magnificent fantasies for strings; most available editions clog Purcell's articulated counterpoint in a bog of nineteenth-century bowings. When Purcell wanted slurs, he put them in; when he did not, he left them out. To over-ride his views seems an impertinence which cannot be excused on the grounds that he would have written his music differently if he had been alive today. Of course he would: but then the music itself would have been utterly different, too; and since we cannot know what changes he would have made either in his music or in its notation, the only thing we can safely do is to assume (a) that he

meant what he wrote; and (b) that he followed the conventions and taste of his time.

(5) Staccato dots and dashes are another frequent source of misunderstanding in modern performances of old music. We have already seen that in music written in the French style, dots over a string of quavers mean not that they are to be played staccato but that they are all of equal length. When the wedge-shaped staccato sign (') is used by composers from Couperin to Beethoven, it never has its modern meaning of staccatissimo, which it acquired only in the early years of the nineteenth century. It is the exact equivalent of the modern staccato dot, and it should be played as though it were one. Editors of old music would be well advised to change the sign into its modern form, for the present-day distinction between the two signs is a valuable addition to the repertory of musical notation; and the accepted meaning of the wedge-shaped dot is so deeply ingrained in the modern player's mind that he instinctively interprets it in its modern sense, no matter how carefully the editor explains that this is not its real meaning.

(6) Present-day methods of fingering are equally ingrained in the modern player's mind, and it would be ridiculous to suggest that he should revert to those in use in earlier centuries. The clock cannot be put back, in this as in other matters, and it is a waste of time and energy to try. But the earlier fingering methods will repay careful study, for they provide clues to many points of interpretation which would otherwise be lost. C. P. E. Bach's *Essay* has a long chapter on correct fingering, and the eighteen pieces included as an illustrative appendix to the first edition are carefully fingered (these are readily available in a reliable edition published by Schott: nos. 2353–4). Couperin's harpsichord tutor is full of detailed fingerings of certain passages in his own music, chosen sometimes because of their difficulty and sometimes because a very definite effect is intended which can only be produced with the fingering he proposes. But these books are not our only source of information, though the subject is too vast to be dealt with here.

(7) The proper way of playing ornaments is another stylistic matter that cannot be more than touched on in the present book. Forty or fifty years ago no concert-performer

bothered his head about them. Today some players still do not bother; others take some trouble to find out what they can about their correct performance; and a few fret and fidget unmercifully, losing their sense of proportion in a vain attempt to differentiate between the styles fashionable in Leipzig during January 1726 and those used in Dresden two months later. This is as absurd as fussing about how Latin was mispronounced by the choir at Cöthen when Bach was there, or trying to reproduce Farinelli's vowel sounds.

The trouble about ornaments is not that there is too little information, but that there is too much. Nearly all the contemporary authorities mentioned so far in this discussion of eighteenth-century style spent much time and many pages debating the nice length of an appoggiatura or the just speed of a trill. Nearly every composer who issued a set of keyboard pieces provided the customer with a careful table showing just how the ornaments should be performed. These tables have provided the modern editor with many problems, and he has not always solved them very well. Some editors make a clean sweep of the ornaments as well as the table; others keep the ornaments but omit the table; others insist on writing out the ornaments in the text, and this—though quite a good idea in itself—tends to plant the music with little thickets of hemi-demi-semiquavers that are far less easy to understand than the original signs would have been. Many of the tables have been reprinted by Dannreuther, Dolmetsch, Wolf, Brunold and others, and some of these experts have discussed the whole problem in great detail; a summary list of the more important signs and their most usual meanings will be found on p. 176 of the present book. Ornaments are delicate, instinctive things; if they are not ornamental they are worse than useless, and anxiety about the right way to play them must never be allowed to cloud a performer's sense of the underlying structure of the music they adorn.

CHAPTER VI

STYLE IN THE SEVENTEENTH CENTURY

THE complex international cross-currents in the musical life of
the seventeenth century: the bewildering array of musical
idioms in use; the rapid fluctuations in musical taste brought
about by the dictates of fashion, changes in the structure of
society, and political upheavals; the unusual variety of technical
difficulty in the music itself, ranging from the very simple to
the extremely advanced; the frequent use of obsolete instruments side by side with those represented in the orchestras of
more modern times; the rarity of the original sources and of
modern editions of them: all these and many other considerations led the nineteenth-century historian to label the period
with the convenient term of 'transitional', which left him free
to continue his researches into the more manageable styles of
the sixteenth or the eighteenth centuries. But during the last
hundred years or so the music of this 'transitional period' has
become increasingly attractive to the average musician as
well as to the scholar. Purcell, Monteverdi and Schütz are no
longer the shadowy and little-known figures they were seventy
years ago; and their music is no longer regarded as merely a
mysterious territory for the musical explorer or as a museum
of interesting archaeological specimens of the kinds of thing
that the eighteenth century did so much better. Some attempt
must be made, however superficial it may be, to review the
considerations of style that were considered important by the
seventeenth-century musician; some of them may legitimately
be dismissed as too fastidious, perhaps, but others cannot be
neglected in the modern performance of seventeenth-century
music.

The first thing to be done is to break up the problem into
smaller pieces, and for the music of this period a chronological
survey will be less satisfactory than one which deals with problems of interpretation encountered in the music of each main

country in turn. The relatively outlying countries such as Spain, Denmark, Poland, Hungary and much of Germany can be linked with the problems presented by the main currents of musical thought: those of Italy, France and, to a lesser extent, England.

ITALY

Italian composers and their music were undoubtedly the dominant influence throughout the seventeenth century, and it is only proper therefore that this survey should begin with Italy. Setting aside pure dance music, a dividing line may be drawn at about 1630; two important styles command the first thirty years of the century, and one equally important style commands the remainder. The first two are Florentine monody, and the Venetian style of the Gabrielis.

The stylistic features of vocal monody (HAM 182-5) govern a great deal of the instrumental music of the same period. Monody was intensely expressive, and the function of the music was limited to that of giving life to every nuance of the words; monody was also intimate room-music, for connoisseurs and amateurs. The phrases the monodists used when writing about their music illustrate the point: 'capable of moving the passions in a rare manner', 'apt to move the passion of the mind', 'the understanding of the conceit and the humour of the words . . . doth more avail than [counterpoint]'. But the special style of passionate singing that the monodists favoured is only to be used in monody:

> Yet by consequence understand, that in *Airy* Musicks, or *Corants* to Dance, instead of these Passions, there is to be used only a lively cheerful kind of Singing, which is to be carried and ruled by the *Air* it self. In the which, though sometimes there may be place for some *Exclamation*, that liveliness of Singing is in that place to be omitted, and not any Passion to be used which savoureth of *Languishment*. Whereupon we see how necessary a certain judgment is for a *Musician*, which sometimes useth to prevail above Art.
>
> (Caccini, 1602, as translated in Playford, 1654)

In the course of this preface Caccini explains in great detail the exact ways in which rubato, dynamics and phrasing should be used in his music in order to enhance its effect. Yet it is unfortunately true that scarcely a single editor or singer of such well-known songs as Caccini's 'Amarilli mia bella' models his or her interpretation on Caccini's own clearly expressed instructions. Monody must *never* be sung as an exercise in bel canto; it is a study in passionate declamation of a highly emotional kind. Of its nature, the instrumental music of the same period cannot set out to stir the emotions in the same way that vocal monody does, and in any case many of its stylistic features derive from an entirely different source (the sixteenth-century canzona). But the mood should be the same, and violin music by Salomone Rossi or Biagio Marini (see HAM 198–9, 210) must on no account be allowed to sound merely like bad Corelli.

The Venetian style of the Gabrielis and their pupils and followers has already been mentioned in Chapter III. The element of space is an essential feature of the music and one that must be reproduced whenever possible (e.g. in performances of HAM 173 and 202). Contemporary accounts give very precise descriptions of the effect of this music on the listener:

In Venice . . . upon Saint Roches day being Saturday and the sixth day of August [1608]. . . . I heard the best musicke that ever I did in all my life both in the morning and the afternoone, so good that I would willingly goe an hundred miles a foote at any time to heare the like. . . . This feast consisted principally of Musicke, which was both vocall and instrumental, so good, so delectable, so rare, so admirable, so superexcellent, that it did even ravish and stupifie all those strangers that never heard the like. . . . Sometimes there sang sixteene or twenty men together, having their master or moderator to keepe them in order; and when they sung, the instrumentall musitians played also. Sometimes sixteene played together upon their instruments, ten Sagbuts, foure Cornets, and two Violdegambaes of an extraordinary greatness; sometimes two, a Cornet and a treble violl . . . and sometimes two singular fellowes played together upon Theorboes, to which they sung also, who yeelded admirable sweet musicke, but so still that they could scarce be heard but by those that were very neare them. . . . At every time that every severall musicke played, the Organs, whereof there are seven faite paire in that room, standing al in a row together, plaied with them.

Thomas Coryat (1611)

On Easter Day [1618] at the cathedral of Santa Maria del Fiore, Florence, Vespers were sung in a setting for four choirs, two of them in the choir stalls and one in each of the organ lofts; His Highness the Duke and the congregation were mightily pleased.

Cesare Tinghi (adapted)

In the Church of the Minerva, Rome, the Vigil and Feast of St. Dominic were celebrated with splendid music. There was one choir in each loft of the two main organs near the altar, and along the nave were eight more, four on each side; these were on stages some eight or nine feet high and about the same distance apart, and facing one another. Each of these choirs was accompanied by its own positive organ. . . . Now a treble from the first choir sang and was answered by those of the third, fourth and tenth choirs; now two choirs would compete with one another, and then immediately two others replied to them. . . .

André Maugars (1639) (adapted)

Perhaps there is no need to emphasize that the word 'choir' in these extracts denotes any ensemble, vocal, instrumental, or mixed. The evidence they provide can be supplemented from Agazzari's valuable little book on continuo-playing, published in 1607. He suggests that each group of performers should be fairly small, and each should have an appropriate continuo instrument. A group of two or three should have a lute, chitarrone, theorbo or harp; a group of six or seven will need a small positive organ or a harpsichord, and a group of sixteen or twenty a large organ or a large harpsichord or both together. The registrations used should match the number of performers; a large group can be accompanied more loudly and more ornately than a smaller group, and in either case the higher voices must never be doubled or obscured. Chords repeated in the middle of a vocal roulade will disturb the singer. The continuo instruments ought to be reinforced by contrapuntal instruments (violins, citterns, and so on) that will extemporize counterpoints above the bass or delicate divisions on the written parts.

But the most stimulating and at the same time the most authoritative suggestions on the performance of music of this kind come from the German organist Praetorius, who was lucky enough to be employed by the most intelligent prince-musician of the early seventeenth century, Maurice, Landgrave of Hesse. The prefaces to Praetorius's numerous (and for the most part rather dull) compositions and his encyclopaedic treatise, *Syntagma Musicum* (1615–19), are a mine of information on the music of his time, whether German, Italian French or English. His keen mind, wide interests and great accuracy in setting down on paper what he knew make him one of the most important musical writers of all time, and no student of early baroque music can afford to ignore what he has to say. Here is a summary of some of his remarks about the Italian music of his time.

(1) Tempo: 'C is slow and ₵ is fast, but look at the music to discover exactly how slow or how fast it should be. Choral music should be much slower than other music; if a song or an anthem is hurried it becomes confused and meaningless. Let there be a gentle rallentando at the end of a piece. Crotchet =80 is a good average sort of speed; *Piano* may mean slow as well as soft. If trumpets are being used in the piece, let the tempo slacken slightly when they are playing and gather a little speed when they are silent.'

(2) Continuo-playing: 'Swift runs and divisions are proper to flue-stops, a simple gravity to regals and reed-stops. Choose the continuo instrument properly; thus trombones should be accompanied on the regal, strings and solo voices on the theorbo or harpsichord, choirs on the organ or large harpsichord.'

(3) Ensembles: 'Reinforce the bass-line with a double-bass or a contra-bassoon, which will give body to the tone. The inner parts may be doubled at the unison or upper octave by an instrument, for the same reason. Try performing a madrigal once on voices, once on instruments, and finally on both in combination. In a long choral work, let there be

an extemporized organ prelude and postlude, and perhaps some interludes as well; or a pavane or solemn madrigal played on the keyboard will do instead. Experiment with sonorities in works that at first glance appear to be *a cappella*; thus for di Lasso's "Laudate pueri" *à* 7, try a combination of two flutes, violins or cornetts, two altos, and three trombones. For his "In convertendo" *à* 8: three flutes (or three mute cornetts; or a violin, a mute cornett, and a flute or recorder; or a boy may sing the top line of all), and a tenor (doubled or replaced by a bassoon or a trombone) for one choir; and voices, viols, violins and cellos, or recorders (with a bassoon for the other. For his "Quo properas" *à* 10, let each choir be composed of one of the following possibilities:

> cornett (or two flutes in unison), four trombones; voices;
> two violins, two violas, and a cello;
> two recorders, two trombones, and a bassoon.

Any of the top four parts can be replaced by a voice if you wish. Wert's "Egressus Jesus" *à* 7 was once performed in my hearing by seven viols, two flutes, two boys, an alto, a violone, two theorbos, three lutes, four harpsichords and spinets, and two citterns, and it sounded very beautiful.'

MONTEVERDI

The kind of performance outlined in the previous section is required for such works as Monteverdi's *Vespers* and his *Orfeo*. Both are written in a rather exaggerated manner in which a large number of different and distinct styles of the time are assembled into one bundle.

In the *Vespers* the chorus, the orchestra and the soloists should never be set out in a single array on a concert platform. The whole body of performers should be split up in the way described by Coryat, Tinghi and Maugars, and scattered in small groups, each with its sub-conductor and continuo instrument(s), throughout a highly resonant building; then this opulent work will sound in its full splendour. Sections in *falso-bordone* are, in the Roman *falso-bordone* tradition, to be sung by a solo quartet, not by a chorus; the obbligato roulades of the soloists and their accompanying instruments must sound as though they are being improvised; the successive sections of 'Ave Maris stella' must reach the listener from different directions. The whole work is designed to dazzle and bewilder the listener in the same way that the architecture of the Counter-Reformation is designed to dazzle and bewilder the spectator. A performance of the *Vespers* with all the performers packed together at one end of a concert hall is comparable with a photograph of a Jesuit church of the early seventeenth century; both have been robbed of two dimensions—mystery, and perspective—and their planned effect is thereby dimmed, even erased.

Though Monteverdi's *Orfeo* is now widely recognized as the masterpiece it undoubtedly is, this work, too, is usually performed with an inadequate realization of the circumstances for which it was written and the surroundings in which it was first heard. The title-page describes it as 'a legend set to music', and both the libretto and the music possess much of the highly stylized and dreamlike quality of a legend. The characters of the story are remote, not men or women, but figures moving in a world of shepherds, divinities and personifications, and the choral writing and orchestration are often as flat and motionless as a piece of stage scenery. The thin stream of rather monotonous recitative is deliberately designed to throw into greater relief the dramatic airs and choruses, and it must be made to sound 'interesting' only when it has some definite dramatic function to perform (HAM 187). The work was first performed by members of a musico-poetic club, and this accounts for many of the details of orchestration as well as for the curious way in which the classical legend is reshaped so that its central theme becomes that of the power of music. The surviving full-score is very laconic in its indications of such important matters as instrumentation, figuring of the bass, tempi and dynamics, and most of the problems of interpretation will therefore be the responsibility of the editor rather than of the performer. Like the *Vespers*, *Orfeo* makes deliberate use of the element of space; there ought to be a body of instruments behind the scenes, some instruments actually on the stage itself, and others grouped in front of the stage and on either side of it. To mass them all together into a single body will not produce the effect Monteverdi had in mind.

These two works have been discussed in some detail for several reasons. They are by a great composer; they are famous and typical examples of early seventeenth-century music at its most splendid; they have become rather fashionable recently; and they tend to be inadequately presented. The principles which ought to govern a present-day performance of them will also apply to much of the ensemble music of this period, whether for church, theatre or chamber; but they will not be of much help to the player of solo music—keyboard music, for instance.

FRESCOBALDI

Frescobaldi is the most important Italian keyboard composer of the early seventeenth century, and the prefaces to his beautifully printed volumes of keyboard and other music (1614–42) contain some very explicit directions on how his music should be played. These make it clear that, once again, the notation in use at this period is an inexact indication of how the music should sound. Since his remarks hold good for much of the music of his time, a summary of them may be helpful; they will in any case apply to HAM 192–4.

(1) In partitas, ricercars and capriccios begin slowly (even if the music is written in quavers), so that later and faster passages may sound more brilliant.

(2) At cadences and trills, slow up and let the trill become slower too. Pause momentarily on the last note of all and then plunge boldly into the next section of the music.

(3) Play expressive sections slowly. Emphasize suspensions and dissonances by lingering over them, and use frequent arpeggios whenever the music shows signs of growing empty.

(4) Simultaneous roulades in quavers and semiquavers should be played dashingly. But when a trill and a roulade occur together in the same note-values, playing them note-against-note will confuse the music; therefore increase the

speed of the trill. In both cases pause a little on the last note of the previous section, since this will make the roulades and trills sound more sparkling.

(5) Roulades with quavers in one hand and semiquavers in the other must not be played too fast; and the semiquavers should be made to sound unequal, the second of each pair being longer than the first.

(6) Sections without roulades should not be too slow. Canzonas are brisker than ricercars and capriccios.

(7) 3/1=adagio; 3/2=faster; 3/4=faster still; 6/4=allegro.

(8) There are two points that Frescobaldi does not explain, perhaps because he thought them too obvious and well known to bother about. They are of the greatest importance in much seventeenth-century music and they must therefore not be omitted here. The figures ♩ ♫ or ♩ ♫ denote trills, even when there is no *tr* or similar sign anywhere near them. And dotted rhythms are often wrongly noted, in Frescobaldi as in Monteverdi:[1] ♪ ♫♫♩ must often be played as ♪ ♫♫♩ (HAM 192, *quarta parte*, and HAM 194) and ♩. ♪♩ as ♪ ♩

The Italian music of the remaining part of the seventeenth century is much easier for the interpreter to handle. The rich diversity of styles of the earlier years becomes melted into the single style of *bel canto* (HAM 203 and others); and though this term is primarily used for describing the vocal music of this time, it is equally applicable to the instrumental music. Everything must sing (except for recitative, which must speak; it is often performed too slowly and too singingly, whether it is by Cesti, Scarlatti or Mozart). The string music of the period calls for a dashing energy in fast movements and an eloquent clarity in slow ones; but it is too little known today to warrant a detailed discussion here.

FRANCE

In the seventeenth century as at so many other times, French music and musical taste differed very considerably

[1] And even Byrd.

from the music and taste of other countries; the most important French contributions to the development of music during this period were the lute-suite, and the operatic style of Lully. Enough has been said already about how to play Lully's music; Lully himself illustrated the difference between the French and the Italian styles of composition and performance as early as 1659 (*Ballet de la Raillerie*) by means of a scene between 'French music' and 'Italian music'. Each of the two characters sings in the proper language and the proper style, and the differences between the two styles are very marked.

But the solo instrumental music of the seventeenth century needs a different approach. A continuous line of development links the lute-music of Gaultier and his school with the harpsichord suites of Chambonnières, d'Anglebert, and Couperin, and many of the mannerisms of the later composers can be traced directly back to the technique and limitations of the lute. We are unfamiliar with the instrument today, and its immense repertory, at least as extensive as the keyboard repertory of the same period, is almost entirely unknown; as a result, we underestimate the size of its contribution to the development of music and misinterpret much music written under its immediate influence.

In the seventeenth century the lute was above all a French instrument; when the lute was used in other countries, its tunings, its tablature and its technique were all adapted from French models. In Italy, for instance, no music in Italian tablature was printed after 1612 and seventeenth-century manuscripts in Italian tablature are almost unknown; the lute itself was soon superseded by the chitarrone and theorbo, and these were accompanying instruments rather than solo ones. In Germany, German tablature was not used after the early 1590s; book-titles like Fuhrmann's *Franco-German Lute* (Nuremberg, 1615) and Mylius's *Treasury of the Graces* (Frankfurt-on-Main, 1622) showed which way the wind was blowing. In England, where in any case French tablature had always been used, the older style represented by the music of Dowland and Holborne suddenly dropped out of fashion in the early years of the reign of Charles I; the lute-music of the middle years of the century slavishly followed the lead set by foreign virtuosi like 'the brave Gotier' (the elder Gaultier, who came to England in 1617 and stayed for many years). Tutors like *The Lute's Apology* (1652) or Mace's *Musick's Monument* (1676) teach a completely Frenchified style and technique. Even the curious uses of the titles of the Greek modes found in Butler's *Principles of Musick* (1636), Farnaby's manuscript 'Psalmes of David' and Playford's *Introduction to the Skill of Musick* (1654) derive from French adaptations of the theories of the sixteenth-century neo-Platonists. These are well expressed in a letter written by the painter Nicolas Poussin; freely translated, this reads:

> The noble Greeks, inventors of everything beautiful, discovered several modes by means of which they produced wonderful effects . . . and it was for this reason that the old philosophers attributed to each of the modes certain special qualities. The Dorian was wise, grave and severe; the Phrygian wild, vehement and warlike (during the next year I want to paint something in the Phrygian mode—some fearful battle scene, perhaps). The Lydian mode was melancholy, the Hypolydian sweet and joyful— suited for celestial, glorious matters. The Ionian was for dances, bacchanals and feasts.
>
> (24th November, 1647)

These rather odd theories about the proper effects of the modes were in wide currency in England, Italy, Germany and France during the seventeenth century (see also p. 129); the titles of the modes were associated with certain keys and key-signatures (though these bore little or no resemblance to the church modes of earlier times), and pieces written in any of the modes were considered to embody the characteristics of that mode, and were to be performed accordingly. Clearly we cannot afford to be ignorant of these theories, since they will play such an important part in the interpretation of much seventeenth-century music.

The first indication of the specially French attitude towards the lute can be seen in the title of Nicholas Vallet's lute-book *The Secret of the Muses* (Amsterdam, 1615–19); but its vogue was at its height in the 1630s, and it is most wonderfully and spectacularly expressed in a famous manuscript lute-tablature (now at Berlin) containing music by the younger Gaultier (HAM 211). The book, *The Rhetoric of the Gods*, is most sumptuously written and illustrated. On the title-page the lute is declared to be 'the arbiter of love, of peace and of war': fantastic attributions, perhaps, to our ears. But even the learned Father Mersenne, whose books about music are among the most important documents of the 1630s, ends his discussion of the lute with:

> A lute-player can do anything he pleases with his instrument. For instance he can demonstrate the geometrical and harmonic means, the squaring of the circle, the proportionate movements of the heavens and the celestial bodies or of the speeds of falling weights: all these and a thousand other things.

Faced with claims of this kind, even a calculating machine might blench.

All the pieces in *The Rhetoric of the Gods* are grouped together according to their modes—which might perhaps more conveniently be referred to as 'moods'—and each group is preceded by a title-page bearing a symbolical representation of the 'mood'. Thus the picture in the Lydian 'mood' shows the interior of a Roman tomb; through the window at the back the tops of cypresses can be glimpsed. Inside the tomb stand two funerary urns attended by mourning Cupids; one carries an extinguished torch, the other plays a muffled kettle-drum. The foreground is rather gruesomely composed of a shawm (traditionally associated with funeral music), a skull, an owl, and a trumpet bearing a rotting banner. The whole picture seems the seventeenth-century equivalent of the artificial horror of *The Mysteries of Udolpho*:

> The *Terror* raised by *Musical Expression*, is always of that grateful Kind which arises from an Impression of something terrible to the Imagination, but which is immediately dissipated, by a subsequent Conviction that the Danger is entirely imaginary.
> Avison (1752)

The intellectual atmosphere represented by this picture and by the contents of the whole manuscript may seem as

neurotic and absurd to us as it did to Molière in his *Précieuses
Ridicules*. The manuscript certainly shows it in its most
extravagant form, for it is difficult for us to hear much difference
between the 'Lydian' music and the music following the picture
of warrior Cupids in the 'Phrygian mood' or the general
rejoicings of the 'Ionian mood'. All the pieces seem equally
artless and faded, and the splintered style of the lute-writing
suggests to the reader amateurishness rather than art.

But this is to wrong Gaultier. No lutenist alive today has
the technique and insight needed to do justice to this highly
romantic music, and it cannot be played with its proper effect
on any other instrument. We are judging the music by its
appearance, therefore, not its sound. The ornaments which
seem fussy on paper gave the greatest delight at the time they
were written; the extravagant expressions of emotion that are
associated with the various moods meant a very great deal to
the player of the 1630s. We have not the evidence for con-
demning the music; all that we can do is to try to discover what
the seventeenth century thought about it, and apply what we
learn to the interpretation of more accessible music written
under its direct influence. There is a great deal of music which
falls into this category, not all of it for keyboard, and not all
of it by French composers.

The initial impetus came from England, it seems. Dowland,
the greatest lute-virtuoso of his time, was a melancholy man;
his ayres, his musical self-portrait ('Ever Dowland, ever griev-
ing'), his internationally renowned song 'Flow my tears'
provide plenty of evidence of this. His contemporary, Anthony
Holborne, gave fantastic titles to many of his pieces: 'Alone
she sits', 'The funerals', 'The night watch', 'The fruit of love',
'The Duke of Milan's Dump' (a dump—HAM 103—was an
elegy in memory of a dead friend). The 'precious' French
amateurs of the lute followed the lead of these men in their
preference for melancholy music, and in their choice of titles:
'The tears', 'The shower of gold', 'Love's despite', 'The tomb
of M. Blancrocher'. The descriptive headings to so many
later keyboard pieces (HAM 216, 265: or 'The mysterious
barriers', 'The little windmills') are direct legacies of the
early seventeenth-century amateurs of the lute.

To sum up, then, the keyboard music of Chambonnières (HAM 212: ornaments omitted!), d'Anglebert (HAM 232), Couperin and the other French composers of the seventeenth and early eighteenth centuries (HAM 229, 231, etc.) must be played with the utmost sensitivity and delicacy of nuance, particularly pieces written in the lute style (preludes, *pièces luthées*). Many pieces of this kind are clearly labelled; those that are not can easily be recognized by their broken figuration, isolated snatches of melody, and wavering texture. Too much emphasis should not be laid on the integrity of the suite as a form; it was originally merely a group of pieces using the same tuning of the lute and arranged together for convenience, and no player should feel that it is his duty solemnly to play through the whole of a suite by d'Anglebert or an 'ordre' by Couperin from beginning to end. Those movements that he likes can be played, and the others can be omitted. The importance of the 'literary' associations of certain keys can perhaps be exaggerated, yet there can be no doubt that many composers and players took them very seriously, and it is thus worth making some effort to recapture them. Speeds must never be excessive; Gaultier particularly warns the player to play slowly in order to avoid the very common fault of muddling the music. Allemandes and pavanes are meditative and even tragic; courantes are more tender and subtle, their rhythm constantly swaying between 3/2 and 6/4. Sarabandes are majestic and balanced; gigues, galliards and even canaries must have no more than a piquant touch of lightness. Arpeggios must be fairly slow, beginning from the bass and with each note clearly defined; their rhythm should be uneven, the upper notes of the arpeggio being delayed for quite a time after the bass has been sounded. Details of this and some other niceties of the same kind may be found in Perrine's book (1680) of harpsichord transcriptions of lute-music (HAM 211). And Perrine, like so many other writers, confirms that in nearly all of the music written in this style 'the first part, or part of a part, of a beat should be longer than the second'—another reminder of the slightly swaying rhythm, superimposed on a steady beat, that should lend such unmistakable charm to every performance of this fragile music.

ENGLAND

Music in seventeenth-century England, as in other countries of Europe, was such a medley of styles and fashions that it would be absurdly pretentious to try to distinguish between them all. But an attempt to summarize some of them may help the performer.

First, the madrigal: this dropped abruptly out of fashion in about 1625 as suddenly as it had risen into prominence in the 1590s. Madrigals are chamber music, ideally performed by no more than one or two singers to a part, and Morley's advice to a pupil who wants to know how to compose them applies to singers who want to know how to perform them:

> You must possesse your selfe with an amorus humor . . . so that you must in your musicke be wavering like the wind, some-time wanton, sometime drooping, sometime grave and staide, otherwhile effeminat . . . and the more varietie you shew the better shal you please.

Compare what Frescobaldi has to say in the preface to his first book of toccatas (1614):

> Do not keep strict time throughout but, as in modern madri-gals, use here a slow tempo, here a fast one, and here one that, as it were, hangs in the air, always in accordance with the expression and meaning of the words.

Canzonets should be sung more lightly, balletts most lightly of all. Instruments may always be used to double or replace any of the voices.

Morley's remarks on the proper tempi of dance-music may be taken to apply to the dance-measures used by the virginalists as well as to the ensemble music for dancing written by Hol-borne, Thomas Simpson, Brade and their German imitators. Pavans are slow and grave, and each section should be repeated either as it stands or else in a varied form. The galliard is lighter and more stirring; the alman is heavier than the galliard, but twice the speed of a pavan. Voltas, corantos and country dances are very brisk.

Motets and fantasies, like pavans, are slow and grave and they were often performed with organ accompaniment, especially during the second quarter of the century. On festival occasions motets were performed with cornetts and trombones added to the ensemble, and a certain amount of music—Adson's book of 1611, for instance—was for a consort of brass instruments rather than strings. Division-viol music, faithful to its Italian origin, should have much of the verve and dash of the Italian style.

Of all the English music of the seventeenth century, the works of the virginalists are perhaps the best known and best loved. The word 'virginalist' is a misnomer; the true virginals had certain tonal features which cannot be reproduced on any other plucked instrument, but the word itself was used for any instrument of the harpsichord family. Virginals music could be played on any instrument that happened to be handy, though some of it is rather better suited to one instrument than to another. Those who play it on the harpsichord ought, perhaps, to remember that (i) in the seventeenth century, leather plectra were unusual; quills give a keener tone than leather, and they demand certain slight changes in the application of the fingers to the keys; (ii) many instruments had only one stop, and very few had more than three; (iii) all stop-changes had to be made by hand. The architecture of the music is complete in itself, and fussy changes of registration will simply blur the nobility and the moulding of the lines.

Many of the questions about tempi have been answered for us already by Morley, and others may be deduced from the time-signatures, which still retained their old connotation of pace as well as metre. Frescobaldi's comments will help, and Playford (1654) has a word or two to say:

₵3 . . . is much used in *Airy Songs* and *Galliards* . . . and is of two Motions, the one slow, the other more swift. The first is, when the *Measure* is by three *Minims* to [the bar]. . . .

The second . . . is to a swifter motion, and is measured by three Crotchets [to a bar]. . . . This swifter *Measure* is used in *Light* Lessons, as *Sarabands*, *Jigs*, and the like.

Playford confirms what we have learned from other sources: dances grow slower as they get older. Sarabandes, corantos and galliards were fast at the beginning of the century and slow by the end of it. It is difficult to transform these sketchy notes from Morley, Playford, and the other writers of the time into metronome marks, and no doubt they would have been surprised to find anyone who proposed to do so. Tomkins (1668) suggested that, for church music, the semibreve is about as long as two beats of the human pulse; this would be considered too slow by our own quick-moving times. (Tomkins is also our authority for the fact that the church pitch of his own time was about a minor third higher than it is today. Chamber-music pitch was about a minor third lower, and madrigal pitch about the same as it is now.)

One or two special features of the notation of the Fitzwilliam Virginal Book and similar contemporary sources may be touched on here.

(1) Francis Tregian, the writer of the Fitzwilliam manu-script, used the symbol :‖: to divide a piece into sections. The symbol may mean a repeat or it may not; the structure of the piece will decide. A three-section pavane may be written as A:‖:B:‖:C:‖: (in which case each section is to be repeated) or as A:‖:A′:‖:B:‖:B′:‖:C:‖:C′:‖: (e.g. FWVB VI), in which case no section is to be repeated since the repeats are already written out in a varied form. In a set of variations or a fantasy (e.g. FWVB I and III) no section is to be repeated. In the smaller dance-forms (almans, corantos, jiggs, toys, and so on) each section ought to be repeated unless, as in FWVB XIX, XX, LIV, it is provided with varied repeats already.

(2) Seventeenth-century composers took it for granted that any player would know how to make the necessary adjust-ments to the text at repeats, but the notation they used may sometimes mislead the modern player. Thus a final chord after :‖: is, as often as not, merely what would correspond to a second-time bar in modern notation; the modern player should be on his guard against making it into a languishing and arpeggiated repetition of the identical chord before the double bar. The last chord of the first section of a piece should usually be held for a full bar on its first playing, being given its

written value only at the repeat. Thus in FWVB CXLV, bar 8, the F♯ in the right hand should be held for four beats the first time, the two quavers at the end of the bar being omitted altogether until the repeat. Conversely, in FWVB CLXXXI, bar 7, the E in the right hand should only be played the first time through; at the repeat the two quavers from bar 15 will be borrowed to lead into the second section of the piece, and when the second section is repeated bar 15 will be omitted altogether.

(3) Ornaments. The exact meaning of the two signs for ornaments (⌒ and ⹀) found in the English sources of keyboard music is still unknown. Different manuscripts containing the same piece commonly show such irresponsible variations in the nature and placing of the ornaments that it is hard to believe they were taken very seriously. Ornaments in Couperin are an integral part of the composer's thought; most ornaments in the English virginalists seem stuck on to the music more or less at random. No contemporary English treatise on keyboard-playing has survived (though one was apparently published in 1597), and much has therefore to be deduced from the practice of such later composers as Locke and Purcell, or from the continental writers like Merulo, Frescobaldi, and Correa de Arauxo who were more or less in touch with the English style. In all probability ⌒ denotes a quick slide up from the third below (or even a measured slide, appoggiatura or 'springer': see p. 176), and ⹀ an upper or lower mordent, trill, or acciaccatura according to the musical context. Merulo (1592) and Diruta (1593) make it clear that at this time *all* mordents and many trills began on the main note (not on the upper or lower auxiliary), and they were not always played on the beat. Here are two great differences between the practice of the early and late baroque period, worth preserving in modern performances. Considerations of fingering will often determine the exact nature of the ornament; there is an interesting article on the subject by R. Beer in *Music Review*, XIII, 1, which approaches the whole problem from a new direction.

It seems that no seventeenth-century manuscripts of viol

consorts contain signs for ornaments. Since they are found in solo music for lute, keyboard and lyra viol, it is difficult to believe that they were not used in ensemble music. Robinson (1603) makes some interesting suggestions for their use in lute music, even when they are not marked, and Playford (1654) and Simpson (1667) give 'a Table of Graces proper to the Viol or Violin'. These are largely derived from the symbols and ornaments used in lute-music, and most of them are especially appropriate to cadences. They differ substantially from the eighteenth-century taste in cadential ornaments, and if ornaments are to be introduced at all into the ensemble music of the seventeenth century, it is as well that they should be the proper ones.

As in Frescobaldi (see p. 111) a trill in consort music is often conventionally written in either of the following forms:

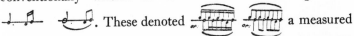

a measured trill, often in a single bow. The existence of this convention can easily be demonstrated by collating sources of virginal music and lute music; its importance to the interpreter becomes clear in, for instance, the opening theme of Ferrabosco's fantasy no. 3 for four viols. What is written as:

should be played as:

Instances of the same convention can be found in early seventeenth-century lyra-viol music, keyboard music and consort music, and it is still very much alive in the music of Locke, Purcell and their contemporaries—yet another instance of a symbol whose original meaning has been obliterated by its modern one.

There was little interruption in English music-making during the Commonwealth, except for church music. Indeed all the signs suggest a quickening interest; the earliest public concerts, the first operatic performances, the revival of music-printing at the hands of John Playford, all took place during the Commonwealth. The Restoration merely deflected the course of a stream that had never ceased to flow strongly. Under Charles I certain foreign influences had made themselves felt here and there: the Frenchified lute-music of the late 1620s, the Italianate 'recitative musick' of Nicholas Lanier, or the Italianisms in Coperario's name (he was born plain Cooper) and work. But the vast bulk of the music written during the reign of Charles I consisted of viol consorts, and these in general remained sturdily English and old-fashioned by comparison with the flighty tastes of circles close to the court. Lawes's songs (HAM 204) were somewhat influenced by the monodists, and they require the kind of impassioned singing prescribed by Caccini. William Young's violin sonatas (1653) were published at Innsbruck, and at first one might be tempted to consider them well away from the main stream of English music. But Young returned to England at the Restoration to become a member of the King's string band, and his viol fantasies show how intimate were his links with the English tradition. His sonatas, in fact, stand midway between the suites of Coperario and the sonatas of Purcell; the fast sections call for brilliance, and the slow ones for a singing style that is completely in the Italian taste. They contain no notational tricks, but ornaments are needed at cadence points and players might like to be reminded that very few of the bowings in the modern editions are by Young himself. Matthew Locke's views on the proper way in which his chamber music should be played have already been quoted (p. 66). His music for masques and plays is written in a slightly different style, but the same general principles will apply.

PURCELL

With Henry Purcell we are on more familiar ground, but his music is an extraordinary mixture of styles, many of them of foreign origin. It would be silly to insist on each of these styles being sharply differentiated from the others in performance; Purcell was after all an Englishman writing in England for an English audience. At the same time, his Italianate music must not be played in a Lullyesque manner and the editor and performer must know what they are about.

First of all, a few words about the instruments he used. 'Flute', for Purcell and his contemporaries, meant 'recorder'. The transverse flute (called 'flute' in the sixteenth century but not in the seventeenth) was considered an outdoor instrument for military men; the flageolet was for the amateur. Purcell's 'hoboy' was the new baroque oboe developed by Parisian instrumentalists like the Hotteterres. It bore little resemblance to the more fiery-toned kind of shawm that was known in late sixteenth-century England as the 'hautboy', and it was in no sense its direct descendant. The 'taille' was a tenor oboe, not a cor anglais. Contemporary oboes, well-played, bear out Bannister's remark that 'with a good reed it goes as easy and as soft as the [recorder]', and it is about time modern historians stopped writing about the old oboe's supposedly intolerable coarseness of tone and began listening to the instrument with their own ears instead of those of the nineteenth century. Like any other instrument it can be played in tune or out of tune, though modern historians again tend to base their opinions on eighteenth-century gossip rather than seventeenth-century sound. The proper bass instrument for accompanying recorders and oboes is the bassoon; any seventeenth-century conductor knew this, and Purcell did not waste time telling him so in his scores.

The strings are more easily dealt with; the 'tenor' is the modern viola (the true tenor violin was tuned a ninth below the ordinary violin and it was demonstrably in use in England during the early years of the seventeenth century, but there is no sign of its ever having been used during or after the Commonwealth). The 'bass violin' was usually tuned a tone below the modern cello; it was very much of an orchestral instrument, and for chamber music the gamba was always preferred. Both the double-bass and the violone were known and used in Purcell's time; once again the double-bass viol was considered more appropriate for chamber music and the double-bass violin for orchestral music. The choice of clefs and the tessitura of the parts suggest that Purcell's magnificent Fantasies and In Nomines were written for a broken consort: viols and violins. A continuo instrument of some kind should be used in any of his ensemble music in which there is a bass part, with the possible exception of these fantasies. 'Possible', for the following reasons: it is clear that in seventeenth-century England a continuo-player was expected to be able to play from a bass-line which was either very sparsely figured or even not figured at all. Agazzari (1607) and Bianciardi (1607) provide the rules for playing from an unfigured bass, and most of them apply to the music of Purcell's time (they will solve many of the problems that have bothered modern editors). Thus the absence of figuring beneath the bass does not necessarily mean that no continuo-player was to take part in the performance. Moreover, copies of works like Young's fantasies à 3 for viols are found both with and without a bass-line for the organ; Purcell's fantasies have survived only in the composer's own autograph full-score, not in sets of parts for performance, and he may well have intended an organ accompaniment to be used.

On the style of continuo-playing fashionable in seventeenth-century England, there is plenty of information ranging from the organ parts to Coperario's fancies or to sacred polyphony, to the treatises of Locke (1673), Mace (1676) and Blow (MS). These may be supplemented by nine contemporary treatises in Italian, German and French, and by various tutors for the guitar (Corbet, Matteis, Derosier), for it is clear that the style was fairly international, varying very little from country to country or from instrument to instrument.

Purcell's table of tempi, published in his widow's edition of his keyboard music (1696), is fairly trustworthy; in addition there are his clear directions in the preface to the trio-sonatas of 1683:

> *Adagio* and *Grave*, which import nothing but a very slow movement: *Presto Largo*, *Poco Largo*, or *Largo* by itself, a middle movement: *Allegro*, and *Vivace*, a very brisk, swift, or fast movement.

The viol fantasies are usually played ridiculously fast by modern string-players, thanks to the heavily over-bowed parts and the injudicious tempi of many editions. The original manuscript contains no bowings at all, and very few tempo indications (which in any case are vague: 'fast', 'drag', and so on). Modern performers will find the works more intelligible if they bear in mind that viols need time to speak, and that Purcell's complex harmony and counterpoint needs time to breathe.

The most Italianate works are, of course, the sonatas of three and four parts for violins, gamba and continuo. The first set (1683) was written in 'just imitation of the most fam'd Italian masters'; the second set (1697) was assembled and published by Purcell's widow, and its style is less Italianate and less clear cut, including such French elements as a chaconne. The abbreviation for a trill mentioned on p. 121 is frequently found, with and without a slur, in both sets (e.g. in the Purcell Society edition, volume VII, p. 45, brace 1, bar 8; 49, brace 3, bar 7; 63, brace 2, bar 7: or volume V, third brace on pp. 7, 10 and 12: or again on pp. 18 and 36); so frequently, in fact, that it is tedious to multiply instances. Cadences will be the better for ornaments (chiefly trills, and usually beginning on the upper note). The notation of dotted rhythms in triple time lacks precision (a distinctive feature of the Italian style, as we have seen already), and these rhythms will often need to be adjusted so as to fit the dominant rhythm of the movement in which they occur. Thus in volume VII, p. 120, the second violin leads off with a trochaic counter-subject to the main theme, and the first violin takes it up a bar later, entering with a crotchet after a crotchet rest. But this version does not match that of the second violin, and it is clear that the rest must be lengthened, and the note shortened, by a quaver. Rhythms of the same kind occur in the very fine sonata in E minor (vol. V, no. VII). Here, on p. 55, brace 2

bar 4, the gamba and continuo lines appear as

Clearly the continuo line must be made to move with the gamba ; consequently we may say that here ♩. ♪♫ means what we would write as ♩. ♪♫. But if this is its proper interpretation here, it cannot help being the proper interpretation elsewhere as well—in the violin parts at bars 2 and 4 of this Largo for instance. Or—more important still—at p. 63, bar 6 of the Poco Largo; if the first violin and the gamba interpret their notation in accordance with this convention, then the second violin must fit with them and ♩ ♪♩ must be interpreted as though it were written ♩. ♪♩. By extension ♩♩ ♪ will often mean ♩ ♩. ♪.

Now this discussion has been elaborate, closely reasoned, and complicated by constant references to the rather inaccessible Purcell Society edition of the sonatas; musical examples are too expensive to include many of them in a book of this size. But it has illustrated Purcell's use of the Italian conventions for the notation of trochaic rhythms; and the music becomes completely transformed when Purcell's notation is correctly interpreted. At p. 171 of this book the reader will find a few bars of this Largo, printed (i) as it appears in every available edition of the Purcell trio-sonatas, from 1697 to the present day; and (ii) in its correct rhythm. These conventional inaccuracies of the Italian style are also to be found in duple time, as we have seen in the previous chapter, and it is not surprising, therefore, to find Purcell using them in duple rhythm also.

It can be shown that the same principles must be applied to rhythms of this kind appearing anywhere in Purcell's music, whether for keyboard, for voices, for wind instruments, or for strings: to the trumpet overture in *The Indian Queen*, for instance, or at the words 'serve the Lord in fear' in the anthem *Why do the heathen rage*, or in the almands and corants of the harpsichord suites. It also applied to the music of his contemporaries and immediate successors—Blow, Croft, Clarke, Eccles and Barrett.

A certain amount of Purcell's music is written in the French taste, and properly speaking this should be performed in accordance with the more important of the conventions used by the players in Lully's band. That Purcell knew Lully's music is certain. He borrowed the tune of an instrumental entrée from *Cadmus et Hermione* for use in *The Tempest*; his Cibell—the prototype of all English cibells—was written in direct imitation of a chorus from *Atys*; and the special vibrato effect used in the Frost Scene from *King Arthur* was first used in Lully's *Isis*, written fourteen years earlier. Moreover, French music had been fashionable in London ever since the

Restoration. The Frenchman, Louis Grabu, was Master of the King's Music from 1666 to 1674; Bannister, his predecessor and rival, had been sent to France in 1661. Gerhard Diesineer, who published a set of instrumental pieces in London in 1680 or so, had been in the French string band at Cassel for many years and his music is extremely French in style. The French composer, Cambert, came to London in 1672 and brought with him Perrin's *Ariane* which was set to music by Grabu and performed two years later. Grabu's opera, *Albion and Albanius* (1685), is mock-Lully (and bad mock-Lully at that); Lully's own opera, *Cadmus et Hermione*, was performed in London by a French company in 1686. The royal string band (The Twenty-four Violins) was founded in direct imitation of Louis XIV's 'Vingt-quatre violons', and we have North's word for it that the overtures, dances and entrées played by the band were wholly in Lully's vein. Purcell's overtures and dances for strings bear the clear impress of the French style, and there can be little doubt that they ought to be performed in accordance with the details given on pp. 78–86; this will involve double dottings in the overtures and the use of the rhythmical French style of bowing—perhaps also the 'rocking' unequal quavers of the French style, though this is less certain, as there is no mention of this trick of interpretation in any published English source of the time.

SOME MISCELLANEOUS MATTERS

(1) *Instrumentation.* For the great part of the seventeenth century instruments of similar tessitura and agility were regarded as more or less interchangeable, as Praetorius's instrumentations for Lassus's motets would suggest; a musical household would have sets of instruments in the various tone-colours, selecting from them freely. Thus the instruments available in 1613 at the court of Praetorius's patron and friend, Landgrave Maurice, included complete consorts of bombards, *schryari*, *bassanelli*, recorders, shawms, flutes, mute cornetts, crumhorns, rankets, Italian viols, English viols, violins, and trombones, with sometimes as many as a dozen instruments to

a set and never less than four. Such outstanding collections as this were of course rare, but they do indicate the rich variety of tone-colours then in use. Composers did not often specify very precisely the exact way in which their music should be performed and the title-pages, sensibly enough, leave the performer plenty of scope. Thus Anthony Holborne's five-part dances (1599) were published for 'viols, violins, or other musical wind instruments'; Brunelli's *Scherzi* (1614) and Rossi's trio sonatas (1607–36) were for violins, recorders or cornetts; most of Frescobaldi's canzonas (1624–34) have no indication of instrumentation whatever; the three melody lines of Schein's *Musica Boscareccia* (1621) could be performed in any of the following ways:

line 1—soprano or tenor;
line 2—soprano or tenor or violin or descant recorder; or even omitted altogether;
line 3—bass voice or trombone or bassoon or violone; continuo optional.

Michael East's viol consorts (1618) were written à 5 and published à 3; J. C. Horn's *Parergon Musicum*, VI (1676), could be played on viols, cornetts, oboes or recorders; and so on. The list could be extended indefinitely, but sufficient examples have been given here to illustrate that in all countries and throughout the century composers were content provided their music was heard, and did not worry too much about the exact sonority that was used. In modern performances of seventeenth-century abstract music (canzonas, sonatas, dances, and so on) we need not be too nice in endeavouring to find players of the ranket or the cornett; as long as the music sounds alive, that will be enough.

Dramatic music, whether for church, chamber or stage, needs more care. Certain wind and brass instruments had particular connotations that they have since lost, and these may be worth recovering. Recorders, for instance, were celestial as well as pastoral; oboes in the early part of the century were funereal, trombones supernatural (a tradition that remains alive in *Don Giovanni*), trumpets and timpani noble and princely, cornetts aristocratic, flutes and drums military. In scoring contemporary music for a masque or play, true authenticity will only be obtained if these connotations are observed.

(2) *Modes and moods.* A little has been said about this subject already in the paragraphs dealing with the French lute-music of the middle of the century. Diruta's directions for organ registration printed in his *Il Transilvano* (1597) and the headings to the modal fantasies in Gumpeltzhaimer's *Compendium* (1611) confirm the wide currency of these ideas in the early baroque period, and it is possible that collections of fantasies in the various modes like those found in Molinaro's lute-book (1599) or Guillet's *Fantasies* (1610) are intended to illustrate these associated moods and should therefore be played in accordance with them. Diruta and Gumpeltzhaimer do not always agree in the moods they attribute to the modes; here is a summary of those upon which they are unanimous:

Mode	Mood	Organ registration		
I	full and serene	16'	8'	4'
II	melancholy and heartfelt	16' and tremulant		
III	mournful and severe	16'	8'	
VI	devotional and soft	16'	8'	
IX	lovely	16'	4'	2'
X	sombre and sad	16'	8'	
XI	lively and agreeable	16'	8'	

(3) *Continuo instruments.* The seventeenth century used these more lavishly than the eighteenth. The orchestra for *Orfeo*, for instance, contained at least thirty-nine instruments and of these no fewer than nine were continuo instruments (though not all of these were used at once). The printed full-score of Landi's *Il Sant' Alessio* (1634) has three melody parts (for unspecified instruments) and two separate bass lines, one for harpsichord and the other for 'harps, lutes, theorbos and string basses'. Cesti's *Ciro* (1664) was scored for strings and five continuo instruments (three harpsichords and two theorbos), and the composer himself was at the first harpsichord for the first performance. Such arrays of continuo instruments would provide a firm rhythmic and harmonic foundation for

E

the orchestra, a wide variety of tone-colour, and a twinkling veil of sound woven into the fabric of the whole work. Some attempt ought to be made to reproduce these characteristic features in a modern performance.

(4) *Expression marks.* The baroque taste for terraced dynamics can easily be exaggerated. There are plenty of instances of strict echo effects in the music of Giovanni Gabrieli, Frescobaldi, Banchieri and Sweelinck; but there are signs that a more sophisticated style had been adopted by the middle years of the century. Thus Mazzocchi's madrigals, printed in score in 1638, contain special signs for piano, pianissimo, forte, *messa di voce*, and a long diminuendo on a sustained chord, and other instances of the same kind are reviewed in Harding (1938). To perform seventeenth-century music too severely is as wrong as to perform it too romantically. The terraced dynamics should be there all the time, but they must never sound dry or automatic.

(5) *Spain and Portugal.* Spanish and Portuguese music of the period from 1550 to 1630 has only recently begun to attract the attention it deserves, and a considerable amount of it is now available in reliable modern editions. Spanish keyboard music of this period is not by any means as isolated from the main stream of music as one might at first suppose, and scholars like Anglés and Kastner have shown that the surviving manuscript sources and printed books are closely linked with contemporary English and, to a lesser extent, Italian styles, and must have been performed in much the same way. Fortunately for the scholar, the Spanish and Portuguese keyboard writers of this time explained in the prefaces to their books many detailed points of style and execution for which there is no other known authority, manuscript or printed, outside the Iberian peninsula; books like those of Santa Maria (1565), Coelho (1620) and Correa de Arauxo (1626) are extremely rare, but extremely important to the student of interpretation. Santa Maria's book belongs to the style of the Renaissance and cannot be discussed here; his remarks on the proper use of ornament are very similar to those of Correa written sixty years later, and there is evidently no intervening break in the Spanish tradition. Correa's preface is wordy (it

takes up thirty-four large pages of the modern edition of his music), but much of his music is so like the work of his Italian, Dutch and English contemporaries that his views on its proper performance can legitimately be applied to theirs.

'The good pupil,' he writes, 'will observe the construction of the music—its peculiarities, its licences, its divisions into solos and accompaniments, its points of imitation, its ornaments, the speeds of its passage work, and so on. Each mode has its special characteristics which must be carefully observed [mode and mood once more. . . !]. In the tablature we use for the keyboard, the lute and the viol, every accidental has to be indicated in the text; there are therefore none of the uncertainties about *musica ficta* that make the performance of vocal music so harassing. The easiest way of playing triplets is to play them evenly; but Cabezón, Rodriguez and other great organists of our time used to play them in a more elegant and gracious way, lingering on the first of each group of three and playing the others rather more lightly. There are three keyboard ornaments: the mordent (*quiebro*), the turn, and the trill (with termination). All should be played quickly, and there is no fixed number of repetitions in a trill; all trills must be semitone trills[1] (except at Phrygian cadences). The sign for the trill is often omitted, but they are nevertheless to be used (i) at all plain cadences leading to a note lasting for a semibreve or more; (ii) on the clavichord, at the beginning of any grave polyphonic pieces whose first note is E or B: on the organ a mordent should be used instead. The turn is proper to the beginning of any solemn piece, or at any melodic step of a second in semibreves or minims when nothing else is happening; it should sometimes be used on crotchets, rarely on quavers, and never on semiquavers. Its lowest note should for preference be a diatonic semitone below the main one. When an ornament is being played, as much of the accompaniment as possible should be taken with the other hand so that the trill may be clear and fast.'

(6) *Fingering*. The fingerings given in Bermudo (1549), Ammerbach (1571), Diruta (1597) and the seventeenth-century

---

[1] The diatonic semitone. Trills will be confined, therefore, to the third and seventh degrees of the scale.

manuscripts of the English virginalists provide a great deal of information on the subject, which cannot be discussed in any detail here. Their instructions are not identical with each other, but the effects they produce are very similar. In Germany and Italy the thumb was little used, and the resulting crossings of the fingers produced an up-beat slurring of pairs of notes in scale passages; in England and Spain the techniques used were rather more modern in feeling (including much greater use of the thumb) and resulted in on-the-beat slurrings in scales. Neither style favoured the monotonously even and effortless legato which we prize today; melodic lines became broken up into little units of two or three notes, and running passages must have been played more slowly and more lumpily than their notation would at first sight suggest to the modern player. Rippling scales and smooth broken-chord patterns are characteristic of eighteenth- and nineteenth-century keyboard techniques; they were neither possible nor, it seems, particularly admired in earlier times, and much keyboard music of the Renaissance and Baroque periods will be reduced to a uniform and mechanical babbling if its figuration is treated in the same way as the figuration of Chopin or Liszt.

Anyone who wants to play early keyboard music with insight must study the effect that contemporary systems of fingering were designed to produce; the resulting phrasings and articulations can then be expressed in terms of the fingering techniques and instruments in use today. Until they do this as a matter of course, many harpsichordists and pianists will continue to make Bull sound like Clementi and Bach like Czerny, and the flow of the music will continue to remind the listener of a running tap rather than a wind-tossed fountain.

CHAPTER VII

THE RENAISSANCE

THE longer the journey back into musical history, the more treacherous becomes the ground on which the interpreter must tread. The sixteenth and earlier centuries have left us no counterpart to the seventeenth- and eighteenth-century treatises dealing with musical taste and style in performance; sixteenth-century books about music are concerned either with teaching the rudiments of music, the complexities of its notation, the techniques of improvisation, and perhaps some smattering of composition, or else with the technical aspects of playing an instrument—fingering, blowing and bowing. They deal in fact with musical theory rather than with musical practice. In spite of its title Morley's fascinating *Plain and Easy Introduction to Practical Music* (1597) is not at all concerned with the practice of music in its usually accepted sense of actual performance, though it does contain a useful hint or two. Holborne's *Cittharn Schoole* of the same year is not even a tutor for the instrument but merely a collection of loosely graded pieces.

Even the theoretical treatises become steadily fewer as we go back in time, and the gap between the written notes and their realization in terms of sound becomes steadily larger and more and more ill-defined. The student of interpretation must rely to an ever-increasing extent on the evidence provided by non-musical sources—painting, sculpture, poetry, chronicles and histories—and, of their very nature, sources of this kind cannot provide him with the coherent and continuous set of data that he really requires. He must piece together his theories from material that was never designed for this purpose, and every scrap of evidence must be turned over and over and carefully tested for its origin, its strength, and its usefulness. The resulting structure cannot be anything but foreshortened, jerry-built and on the verge of collapse, but it is better than nothing.

THE SOURCES

Except for an occasional score published primarily for instructional purposes full scores were quite unknown during the Middle Ages and Renaissance. Printed music was a luxury, and an expensive one at that. It is unfortunately very difficult to find out the contemporary cost of a sixteenth-century music book or the factor by which this should be multiplied to give its equivalent in modern money. A set of vocal part-books of the late sixteenth century might have cost the equivalent of between 30s. and £2, and at the beginning of the century perhaps six times as much. Morley's *Introduction*, bound in full leather, probably cost something like £5 10s. (in modern currency); Petrucci's incomparable music-books were quite as expensive as the modern limited edition from a private press, and only the rich music-lover or bibliophile could have afforded to buy them. Unless they were extremely luxurious, manuscript copies were in general rather cheaper, and these are often the only form in which the music has survived to our own time. But not all manuscripts (nor all printed books) are perfectly accurate; music copying has never been an easy thing to do, and the sixteenth century was no better at it than we are. Moreover the task of the sixteenth-century copyist was complicated by the conditions under which he worked, the greater difficulty of the notation, the relatively high prices of paper, parchment and ink, and so on. Indeed the high cost of writing materials has much to do with the fact that scarcely any autograph manuscripts of the sixteenth or earlier centuries are known to exist today. Most composers made use of what were called *cartelle*: blank sheets of parchment or paper, incised with a dozen or more sets of stave-lines. A polyphonic composition would be drafted on these in pencil or ink; a set of parts could then be prepared from this score; and finally the original text could be erased with a single sweep of a wet rag or sponge, leaving the sheets clean and ready for future use. It is hardly surprising that no specimen of a *cartella* or composing sheet is known to exist today, for they would have been used over and over again until they fell to pieces and were thrown away. But the evidence for their existence survives, even though only in the form of scattered and ambiguous references here and there. Indeed, the very fact that medieval and Renaissance full scores and autograph manuscripts are virtually unknown is almost a good enough argument in itself for the use of some device like a composing sheet; polyphonic music can be composed only with the aid of some kind of score, even by the greatest masters, and it is idle for anyone to suppose otherwise.

Full scores of renaissance music, then, are extremely rare and composers' own manuscripts are, for all practical purposes, non-existent. The editor has to rely on sets of part-books or on choir-books; but even when sources of this kind were prepared under the personal supervision of the composer they cannot have the authority provided for music of the seventeenth and later centuries by autograph manuscripts, by corrected proof-sheets, or by books printed from plates engraved by the composer himself. Moreover a set of part-books may become quite useless if one or more of the books of the set has been lost or destroyed. Years of experience are needed before an editor can restore even a single missing polyphonic line with any sort of confidence that his version is something like the original; to restore more than one is a virtually hopeless task, and failing a lucky concordance with some other source, the surviving fragments may often be utterly valueless to the editor and to the performer (though not, perhaps, to the scholar). Such is the case with the splendid collection of *XX Songs* published in London in 1530; the *bassus* part-book has survived in a single copy, the *tenor* part-book is lost altogether, and of the *triplex* and *medius* part-books only the title-pages are known. One of the pieces in the book is found complete in a contemporary manuscript, but the other nineteen are tantalizing and useless fragments.

The alternative to the set of part-books was the choir-book, in which all the polyphonic parts were set out separately on the open page. These are of course far easier to work from, but they have often survived only in a sadly mutilated state. Some earlier antiquaries valued them only for the illuminated letters they contained, not hesitating to snip these out and paste them in a scrap-book. Others were disposed of as book-binder's scrap a few decades after they were first written; books sent for repair in modern times have sometimes revealed sections of a musical manuscript used in this way, and no doubt there are many other fragments of early music tucked away inside old bindings. If early musical sources were more plentiful these fragmentary remains would be of less interest; but such a prodigious number of manuscripts and printed books have been destroyed by the hazards of time, chance and hatred that these manuscripts often turn out to contain music that would otherwise be unknown.[1]

Even when all the component parts of a composition have survived intact, the editor's task is far from light. It has already been pointed out that in vocal music the words were often either omitted altogether or else set out under the music in a very arbitrary and careless way. In printed music of the sixteenth century both verbal and musical texts were set up from movable type, and it was not always practicable to set a syllable exactly under the notes to which it was to be sung. Several continental printers and one or two English ones did what they could to help the performer; for instance, East's house practice was to set a very small section of blank stave (often no more than a millimetre wide) between the last note of one syllable and the first of the next. But such attention to detail was by no means the rule, and many of the sumptuous liturgical part-books and choir-books issued by printing-houses like those of Plantin in Antwerp or Gardano in Venice do not provide a faultless text, for all their elegant appearance. The editor will find valuable information on the problems of underlay in the treatises of Zarlino (1558), Vicentino (1555) and Tigrini (1588); but even these authorities will not solve all his problems, and they are useless for the music of an earlier generation than their own.

Underlay is not the only problem. Many accidentals were missed out altogether, not through carelessness but because

---

[1] It has been reliably estimated that about half of all the surviving music written before 1600 is now known only from a single manuscript or printed source.

the singing rules of the time would have left the performer in no doubt as to how they should be supplied. The notations used for lute tablatures were far more precise than staff notation in this respect, since each intersection of string and chromatic fret on the neck of a lute was represented by a separate and distinct symbol; lute-transcriptions of vocal music will thus supply many of the accidentals that were lacking from the vocal texts, and no scholar dare ignore the evidence they provide. But even these transcriptions have to be used with great care. It is as easy to make mistakes in writing or printing lute-tablatures as in any other kind of musical notation; moreover, the men who made the transcriptions were not necessarily working from a good text in the first place. Even if they were lucky enough to have a good text in front of them, they were usually players rather than singers, and it was only the sixteenth-century singer who was thoroughly at home in the rules of *musica ficta* and the mazy ways of proportional notation; the player was less highly trained and the style of his music was less complex, but more up to date. The wise editor will keep a very open mind when it comes to making use of lute-transcriptions in the preparation of his own text of a sixteenth-century vocal work; they should be thought of as suggestions, not commands.

The editor's task is still not at an end. The duration of those accidentals that are actually found in the source was governed by a whole complex of interlocking rules which were perfectly familiar to the sixteenth-century singer but have long since been forgotten. The interpretation of certain conventions of notation (rests, ligatures, and so on) was not internationally standardized in the sixteenth century. Plainsong intonations and interpolations were usually omitted since they, too, varied from country to country and even from diocese to diocese. Instruments could be used more or less at the discretion of the musical director of any particular performance; they might replace the voices or they might double them, or in certain circumstances and at certain times in the year the over-riding claims of the liturgy might forbid their use in sacred music altogether. But none of these problems is revealed by the study of the musical texts alone; the careful

E*

scholar becomes aware of them only when the texts are examined in the light of contemporary evidence, and the incautious one will not be aware that they even exist.

No tempo marks are found. The time-signatures used were themselves an indication of the proper tempo of the piece, and the living tradition of the time—long dead—would resolve any doubts. There was no accepted standard of pitch, and the choice of clefs for the various parts might at times indicate that the whole work was to be performed at quite a different pitch from that at which it was written down. Dynamic markings of any kind are utterly unknown during the six centuries that separate the plainsong notation of the tenth century from the Venetian music of the 1590s. The slur had not yet come into use, nor had such refinements of articulation as the staccato dot or the portato sign. The bar-line had been invented, it is true, but it was used only in solo music for keyboard or lute and in study scores (text-book examples, for instance). Very short note-values were not yet in use, and semiquavers or demi-semiquavers could be shown only as longer notes with a special time-signature implying that the time was to be doubled or even quadrupled in speed. The most complicated problems concern the actual durations of the notes. In the music of our own time the relative length of a note-symbol is absolute; in the music of the first part of the sixteenth century (and indeed in much later music as well) the length of a note depended on its surroundings, and a single symbol like a breve might contain anything from eight crotchets to eighteen.

At this point we may well say with the nineteenth-century historian Kastner:

> Dans cette étude laborieuse et ingrate, mais pleine de séduisants mirages, on traverse des déserts pour arriver à des ruines.

Kastner was writing of archaeology, but his remark is perfectly true of medieval and renaissance music. And just as in archaeology the happy amateur sometimes enjoys himself at the expense of later and more scientifically minded students, so in this music the amateur musicologist who gets there first may unwittingly scatter dust and derision in the eyes and ears of his public. The older the music, the narrower the market for modern editions of it: there are enough mirages in the desert already, and the dust devils edited out of nothing by the well-intentioned Mr X or the crystal-gazing Dr Y and spun into motion by their enterprising publishers are all too apt to mislead the novice and exasperate his guide.

But the main concern of this book is with the process of turning notes into sounds, not words into metaphors; and editors are much less interesting persons than performers. It will be convenient once again to consider the problems of interpreting Renaissance music country by country, and Italy must head the list.

ITALY

A comparison of the nineteenth-century edition of Palestrina's complete works with the recent Italian one will show the great advances that have been made in an editor's ability to handle the problems of notation, *musica ficta* and underlay; and a great deal of the music composed and published in sixteenth-century Italy is now available in reliable modern editions (though there is still plenty of it waiting for the musical explorer). Certain conventions of performance are more difficult to elucidate, and some of them may never be wholly recaptured.

Some account has already been given of the sonorities that were dear to a man of renaissance Italy: sparkling organs, lightly winded; whole consorts of one tone-colour; broken consorts of richly contrasting colours; extravagance and pageantry in music as in the other arts and in the life of society. Florence and, later on, Venice were the two societies on which so many others modelled themselves, and it is to the records of Florentine celebrations that we must turn for information on the musical activities of the time. It must be emphasized that the groups of instruments and singers used on these occasions were assembled because they happened to be available and because they made a brave show, not because the

composers insisted that this was the only way in which their
great thoughts could be expressed. Provided that the music
sounded well and looked reasonably expensive, the patron
was satisfied; a composer who behaved as self-centredly as
Beethoven or Wagner would have been thought intolerably
conceited and ill-mannered.

There are abundant records of music-making in Florence
under the Medicis, and here are some selected extracts from
them, arranged chronologically.

1539: for the wedding of Duke Cosimo I and Leonora of
Toledo.

(1) Open-air music to welcome the duchess into the city:
an eight-part motet, sung by a choir of twenty-four and played
by four cornetts and four trombones.

(2) Indoor music (incidental music to an after-supper
play): a madrigal à 4 (Dawn) sung by a soprano accompanied
by a harpsichord and a positive organ; a madrigal à 6 (Shepherds) sung by six shepherds and repeated with the voices
doubled (or perhaps replaced) by crumhorns; another à 6
(Sirens) sung by three sirens and three sea-nymphs, accompanied by three lutes; another à 4 (Silenus) sung by a tenor
accompanying himself by playing the other three parts on
a large viol; a madrigal à 4 (Nymphs) sung by eight hunting
nymphs; another à 5 (Night) sung by a voice accompanied by
four trombones; finale à 4 (Satyrs and Bacchantes) sung and
danced by eight characters, with various accompanying
instruments.

1565: for the wedding of Prince Francesco and Giovanna,
Queen of Austria.

Indoor music to an allegorical play, for sixteen voices and
an orchestra of eighteen players.

(1) Madrigal à 8 (Venus) sung by eight voices accompanied
behind the scenes by two harpsichords, four bass viols, an alto
lute, a mute cornett, a trombone, and two recorders.

(2) Madrigal à 5 (Love) sung by five voices and accompanied behind the scenes by two harpsichords, an archlute, a

bass viol, a treble viol, a recorder (the viols and the recorder extemporized their parts), four flutes and a trombone.

(3) Madrigal à 4 (Zephyrus and Music) sung by four voices with four lutes, a viol, and a lirone on the stage; and accompanied behind the scenes by three harpsichords, an archlute, a treble viol, an alto flute, a large tenor recorder and a mute cornett (extemporizing its part).

(4) Madrigal à 6 (Tricksters) sung by eight voices (treble and bass doubled), and accompanied by five crumhorns and a mute cornett.

(5) Madrigal à 6 (Discord and his Followers, including two Cannibals) sung by a dozen voices with two trombones, a dulcian, two cornetts and a tenor cornett, and two drums.

(6) Madrigal à 5 (Psyche) sung by a soprano with four viols, and accompanied behind the scenes by a lirone and four trombones.

(7) Finale à 4 (Olympus) sung 'very loudly and cheerfully' with four voices to a part, accompanied by two mute cornetts, two trombones, a dulcian, a treble crumhorn, a lirone, a treble rebec, and two lutes.

1567: carnival for the baptism of Prince Francesco's daughter.

Open-air music: masquerade (Hunters) à 6, sung by a dozen voices accompanied by two cornetts, two crumhorns and two trombones; masquerade (The Widowers' Coach) à 6 accompanied by two viols, two trombones, two flutes and two lutes; pageant (Juno, Nymphs and Roman Heroes) à 6, accompanied by two trombones, two lutes, a lira, a harpsichord, a cornett and a flute; masquerade (Butterflies) à 4, first sung *a cappella* and then repeated with trombones and cornetts.

1569: Striggio's 40-part motet (the music still survives) performed by an ensemble of eight trombones, eight viols, eight recorders, two choirs of eight voices, a bass lute and a harpsichord.

Further festivities took place in 1576, 1585 and 1589 and full accounts of the ensembles that took part in them are still in existence. Much of the music used for these magnificent ceremonies has been lost; the madrigals and motets that have survived are usually to be found in manuscript or printed collections which give not the slightest hint that their contents could ever have been performed in such an elaborate way. But the evidence of the festivities is conclusive; madrigals of this kind could be performed in two entirely different manners, the one straightforward, the other highly coloured and including additional extemporized harmony and counterpoint. If we gauge the worth or effectiveness of these works on performances of them in their simple form alone, we may easily misjudge their composers.

To transform these madrigals into their elaborated versions will not be easy. It is clear from the above descriptions that the sonorities used varied with the acoustical surroundings in which the music was heard and with the allegorical personages involved in the performance. Writers like Ortiz (1553) illustrate the techniques of improvising an extra part, and Bianciardi (1607) can be taken as a guide to the style of the continuos. The number of continuo instruments mentioned as taking part in the festivities suggests that continuo instruments of one kind and another were at least as popular in the sixteenth century as they were in the following one; certainly Bianciardi's rules (slightly modified) would have made it possible for anyone to extemporize a continuo from the unfigured bass-line by itself. The rules work if they are applied to the bass-lines of most music written between about 1530 and 1600 or so, as anyone can verify for himself, so that the absence of any printed or manuscript parts specifically marked 'for organ' or 'for harpsichord' can be easily explained. And there was no need for the player to figure the bass; this only became necessary when the harmonic innovations introduced by the composers of the last years of the sixteenth century caused the rule-of-thumb methods described by Bianciardi to break down. Evidence for their use can be found in such writers as Bermudo (1555), who points out that there are three ways of playing the organ: from a part-book, from a score (only for beginners) or from tablature (only for solos). They will be found to work for the unfigured basses given by Ortiz (1553), designed to be harmonized at sight by a harpsichordist while the gambist extemporized divisions above them. Unfigured *basso seguente* parts (giving the keyboard-player the lowest sounding line of the music) still exist for the 40-part motets of Striggio and Tallis, and the rules apply to these as well. In a word, then, Viadana, Peri and Caccini did not invent continuo-playing; they invented the figured bass, which is a different thing altogether. The art of extemporizing a continuo part from an unfigured bass dates back at least to the early years of the sixteenth century, and it was a familiar feature of many sixteenth-century performances. *A cappella* singing and playing was certainly in use, but to nothing like the extent that the musical sources would at first sight suggest.

So much for two of the favourite sixteenth-century techniques of extemporization: once we realize that they existed, our conception of the proper sound of sixteenth-century music becomes considerably transformed. But a third technique was also in use; it is quite as neglected in our own times as the others, but it transformed the texture of sixteenth-century music even more drastically. This technique was the extemporized ornamentation of a written polyphonic part; it was very much in fashion among singers and instrumentalists in the larger cities, and a considerable number of surviving treatises on the subject dating from 1535 to the end of the century show that the fashion was both widespread and longlasting. These treatises suggest that we shall obtain a false impression of sixteenth-century polyphonic lines if we merely reproduce them note for note as they are written. One of the most fascinating of them all was written by Girolamo dalla Casa, musical director of the Venetian State Wind-band, and it was published in Venice in 1584; it includes examples of some well-known madrigals as they would sound with extemporized divisions introduced into all of the parts. An extract from dalla Casa's divisions on Cipriano de Rore's 4-part madrigal 'A la dolc' ombra', together with the plain text, is given on p. 173. Dalla Casa also deals with the special technique of playing the *lyra bastarda*, in which a polyphonic texture was dissolved into a flurry of runs and leaps for a solo bass-viol; at a later date the *lyra bastarda* was introduced into England by Alfonso Ferrabosco II and the eccentric Tobias Hume, becoming known as the lyra viol.

This technique of improvised division was not considered as something to be applied mechanically and indiscriminately. Many writers—Ganassi, for instance—enjoin the player to use graces sparingly, to perform them expressively, to avoid them at the very beginning of a piece, and never to allow them to occur in two parts simultaneously. Nor were they confined to secular music. The virtuoso singers of St Mark's, Venice, or St Peter's, Rome, prided themselves on their ability to extemporize divisions in the performance of church music (a tradition which was still very much alive in the eighteenth and nineteenth centuries—Burney, Mozart and Mendelssohn wrote with admiration of the *abbellimenti* used by the Sistine choir in their performances of Allegri's 'Miserere'), and Bovicelli's printed divisions on some of Palestrina's motets are still extant. They are very like dalla Casa's, and both books may appear rather shocking to us at first. But they illustrate with great clarity the nature of the creative contribution that the sixteenth-century performer was expected to make to the work he was playing or singing, and they show how startlingly wrong our views on sixteenth-century polyphony will be if these are based exclusively on the look of the music instead of on its sound in contemporary performance. Once we have grown accustomed to the idea that extemporization of every kind was an integral part of the performance of early music, we shall be nearer to seeing it in its historically correct perspective and more critical of many accepted opinions about it.

FRANCE

Three sentences will do. French chansons are not Italian madrigals, and they must not sound like them. The same characteristic differences between French and Italian tastes in music that we have already encountered in the seventeenth and eighteenth centuries were in existence in the sixteenth century, and a discerning performance will take account of them. Elegance, nimbleness, wit, restraint, precision in French music: pomp, brilliance, humour, passion, extemporization in Italian music.

GERMANY AND THE LOW COUNTRIES

(1) In the second half of the sixteenth century and the early years of the seventeenth, a number of imported styles (principally Italian or French) were adopted by composers in Germany and the Low Countries. The easiest way for the interpreter to recognize them is by their titles (fantasia, passamezzo, villanella, 'rimes françoises et italiennes', chanson, and so on); they were deliberate attempts at imitating foreign styles, and they must sound as if they were.

(2) Instruments were more freely used in German music than might appear to be the case from the evidence of the musical sources alone. Germans wrote the first treatises to give full illustrations and descriptions of musical instruments— Virdung (1511), Agricola (1528–9)—and the earliest tutors for the organ, lute and viol are German or Austrian—Schlick (1511), Judenkünig (1523), Gerle (1532–3). Most of the fine (and, in England, too neglected) polyphonic songs of the first half of the century were originally written for tenor or soprano voice, accompanied by three or four viols or other instruments, and this leading part must be looked for and emphasized in performance. The title-page of Arnt von Aich's song-book (Cologne, 1519) reads: 'In this little book are seventy-five fine songs to be bravely sung by four voices or to be cunningly played on recorders, flutes and other musical instruments'; but words are underlaid to the music in the tenor part-book alone. The same is true of Schöffer's songs (1513), and of many written or published by Forster, Senfl and their contemporaries. These songs were often performed entirely on instruments, as the title-page of von Aich's book suggests; at Copenhagen there is a set of part-books dating from 1541 containing songs to be played on three crumhorns and a trombone (for the tenor line), four crumhorns, and four cornetts and four trombones. A set of printed part-books (1552) now at Ulm has manuscript directions for the use of flutes, recorders and bagpipes in certain of the numbers. Most of this music, though, will sound at its best on a broken consort of instruments and voices.

(3) A rich selection of different tone-colours was available,

particularly in those towns—and there were many of them—
that prided themselves on their town-bands. At Frankfort-on-
Oder the municipal bandsmen were particularly lucky since
they could choose from among consorts of trombones, dulcians,
recorders, flutes, bombards, shawms, crumhorns, cornetts and
fiddles; but even at a small town like Oudenarde the bandsmen
could choose between consorts of recorders and crumhorns
(two quartets of each, at different pitches) for indoor music,
and they had louder instruments for use in the open air. Bands
like these not only played for civic ceremonies and feasts, but
also provided curfew music from the town watch-tower nearly
every night of the year. Most bandsmen were expected to be
able to play at least four different instruments, and their
repertory ranged from pure dance-music to settings of plain-
songs and chorale tunes.

(4) Extemporized divisions were introduced into German
ensemble music in imitation of the Italian style and, to a
lesser extent, in continuation of the older German tradition
of ornamented keyboard-transcriptions of vocal music. Divisions were used both in Catholic and Protestant Germany—see
Coclico (Nuremberg, 1552) and Finck (Wittenberg, 1556)—
and as early as 1528 Agricola wrote that all instruments ought
to imitate the ornaments and divisions characteristic of organ
music. Once again, therefore, there is a great difference between
what the modern lover of old music sees in front of him, and
what the sixteenth-century musician heard.

ENGLAND

Again there are some important considerations of style
that are not immediately apparent from the surviving musical
sources alone.

(1) In England as in Germany there was a strong sixteenth-
century tradition for the performance of songs by one voice
and a group of instruments. Much of the music written in this
form has perished; Peter Warlock and Dr E.H. Fellowes have
transcribed and edited much of what remains. The tradition
seems to have lost its force in the last quarter of the sixteenth

century, but traces of it are to be seen in Byrd's preface to his first song-book (1588):

> ... heere are divers songs, which being originally made for Instruments to expresse the harmonie, and one voyce to pronounce the dittie, are now framed in all parts for voyces to sing the same.

These songs of Byrd's are rarely performed in their original form even though many of them sound very much better this way. Many later madrigal books were published as 'apt for viols and voices', and though this often seems to have been little more than a conventional phrase, certain works are undeniably more effective performed by a broken consort. Dowland's partsongs are a case in point; the inner parts are often crowded and unvocal, and will sound far more effective on viols or violins.

(2) The English madrigal is chamber music, and even when madrigals are performed by a fairly large choir they must never lose their intimate and varied quality.

(3) No sixteenth-century English treatises on improvised divisions survive, and it is probable that none were written. But it is fairly clear that divisions were used, even if to a much lesser extent than they were on the Continent. A few remarks in Morley (1597) suggest that some choirmen were in the habit of adding extempore runs and cadences to the music in front of them, and many of the variant readings recorded in the ten volumes of *Tudor Church Music* seem to have originated in this way (see p. 172). For instrumental music the evidence is more elusive, but the varied repetitions that characterize so many of the pavans and galliards of the virginalists are also found in collections of solo lute-music and in the elaborate *Consort Lessons* for six instruments by Morley (1599–1611) and Rosseter (1609); and it is difficult to believe that similar varied repetitions were not introduced extempore in dance music for instrumental consorts by men like Holborne, Simpson, Brade and the younger Ferrabosco. One example may be found in British Museum Add. MS 31390, ff. 80'–81 (Parsons' *De la Court Pavan*, with elaborately ornamented

alternative endings to the last section), but written-out divisions of this kind are extremely rare.

(4) The inventory of Henry VIII's musical instruments suggests that as lavish a selection of tone-colours was available in England as elsewhere. Many of the larger country houses (Hengrave Hall, for instance, where Wilbye worked for many years) had substantial collections of musical instruments for household music-making; important cities like Norwich or York had their own civic bands, and Erasmus mentions that he heard music admirably performed in church by an ensemble of voices and instruments (probably cornetts and trombones). To perform all Tudor music *a cappella* is to see it in black-and-white instead of in the rich colours that the contemporary listener seems so often to have preferred.

(5) Fa-burden—the English technique of extempore harmonization—can be traced back at least to the beginning of the fifteenth century. A casual remark of Morley's—'as for singing uppon a plainsong, it hath byn in times past in England (as every man knoweth) and is at this day in other places, the greatest part of the usuall musicke which in any churches is sung'—shows that the technique was very far from obsolete in his lifetime. Yet since it was wholly extemporized, no trace of it is to be found in the musical sources of the sixteenth century; once again, to rely merely on the written musical symbols is to build up a misleading picture of the music of the time.

(6) The sources of most of the plainsongs used in English music before 1600 may be found in the liturgical books of Sarum and, to a lesser extent, those of more local Uses such as York and Hereford. Much fifteenth- and sixteenth-century polyphony was designed to have plainsong interpolations or introductions: the intonations to the various sections of the Mass, for instance, or the alternate verses of hymns, Te Deums and Magnificats. These plainsong excerpts are usually omitted in the sources of polyphonic music, and they have been omitted in most modern editions; but they will need to be restored in any performance that claims to be authentic. No one knows very much about how plainsong was sung in the sixteenth century. One thing is certain; it was not sung in

accordance with the theories of Solesmes, which were developed in the late nineteenth century after careful investigation of the notations used in the twelfth century. Plainsong sung in the Solesmes style sounds very well; but it is hopelessly anachronistic to associate this style of singing with the polyphony of the fifteenth and sixteenth centuries. Plainsong hymns were almost certainly sung in a strongly marked and swinging triple time. The notation used in certain fifteenth- and sixteenth-century manuscripts of plainsong and polyphony, in Marbecke's 'Anglican' plainsong, and in theoretical books on composition would seem to suggest that other plainsong, too, was sung metrically in the sixteenth century. But the subject is a difficult and delicate one, and so far few scholars have studied it.

CHAPTER VIII

THE MIDDLE AGES

THE present-day performance of music written between 1100 and 1500 presents the students of interpretation with immense problems, many of which will probably never be solved. Medieval musical instruments have nearly all been destroyed, and very few writers described them in sufficient detail to enable them to be reconstructed with any certainty. The further we go back in time, the more allegorical become the paintings and the poems and the less satisfactory the conclusions that may be safely drawn from the evidence they present. Theoretical writers become increasingly pedantic and obscure, musical sources rarer and rarer, musical notation less and less exact; and the music itself seems ever more remote and detached from our normal musical experience. But the fact remains that medieval music is being performed today (a fact which would have surprised its composers very much indeed), and something therefore must be said about its interpretation. The medieval composer's approach to the problems of musical composition and performance was so radically different from the approach of nearly all the composers of later times that his music needs to be handled very carefully if it is not to be completely misunderstood.

In the Middle Ages a composer wrote the individual voices of a polyphonic composition successively, not simultaneously; he put music together, in fact, which is what the word 'composition' properly means. He began with the tenor (the 'holding part'); this was the core round which the whole piece was to be constructed and it had therefore to be fine, well-made, and complete in itself from beginning to end. When he had finished writing the tenor, but not before, the composer set to work on the *discant*—a counter-melody making good two-part counterpoint with the tenor throughout; this part, too, was polished and perfected until it was to the composer's liking. Then he began on the third part, most commonly called the *contratenor*, which wove the other two parts together into a firm whole. Once the contratenor was completed, he was free to add another part (if he felt so inclined) and after that, yet another.[1] Now this technique of composition leads to one very important result: the music is complete in one part or in two parts or in three. The tenor may be performed by itself; or tenor and discant may be performed together; or the contratenor may be included as well. A music-loving household that could not muster enough resources to perform music in three parts could omit the contratenor altogether without doing much damage to the music; on the other hand, no composer would feel the slightest hesitation in writing a couple of additional parts to somebody else's three-part work in order to make full use of the performers at his disposal. Indeed he would probably feel rather pleased with himself; on the evidence of much fifteenth-century writing about music, it would seem that the musician who was able to create new music out of old was considered rather cleverer than someone who merely spun completely new material out of his own head.

These re-workings of other men's music are a very characteristic feature of much fifteenth-century music, and they often make it very difficult for the scholar to state categorically that this or that version of a particular work is the definitive one. Often a whole piece of music is found ascribed to the man who merely wrote one of the optional extra parts. Thus in British Museum Add. MS 31922 there is a fine four-part piece, 'Gentyl prince de renom' by 'the Kynge H. viij'; but, unfortunately for Henry's musical reputation, hard-headed scholars have had to narrow down his share in the music to a fumbling and repetitive alto part, for the other three parts appeared in print in Venice when he was only a boy of nine. And this is only one of very many examples of the same kind.

The implications of all this for the performer are con-

---

[1] For the sake of clear presentation this account has been simplified, but it is substantially accurate. In secular songs the discant was often written first and the tenor added later.

siderable. He must make certain that the main melodic line is clearly defined and that the others remain subordinate to it. On occasion one or more of the subordinate lines may even be better omitted altogether.

TEMPO

The student of medieval music cannot turn to contemporary writers like Quantz or L'Affilard for help with the problem of deciding the proper tempo for a piece. A few theorists discuss it, to be sure, but usually as part of their explanation of time-signatures or of some new feature of notation that they are anxious to see standardized, and their explanations are often wordily and incoherently expressed in very monkish Latin. For many years the problem was burked by scholars altogether, but recently one or two (notably Apel and Besseler) have made some attempt at expressing the information provided by these theorists in terms of modern metronome marks; their suggestions are necessarily very tentative but they are at least a beginning.

c. 1200	long= 80	
c. 1250	breve=120	
c. 1280	breve= 80	
c. 1320	semibreve=120	
c. 1350	semibreve= 80	
1400–1500	semibreve= 50	in time-signatures of O or C
,,	=100	,, ,, ,, Φ or $\mathbb{C}$
,,	= 70	,, ,, ,, C_2^3
,,	=140	,, ,, ,, C3 or $\mathbb{C}$ $\frac{3}{2}$

This table illustrates very clearly the way in which the duration of any note-value has become longer and longer as the centuries progress—a tendency which has continued uninterruptedly up to our own time, and one that completely justifies the reduction of the note-values used in earlier music to their modern equivalents.

It must be emphasized that these markings are very far from definitive or precise. They take no account of the differences in notation and style between French and Italian music of the fourteenth century, for instance, or between English, French and Flemish music of the late fifteenth century. But subtleties of this kind are next to impossible to re-establish some four centuries or more after they have passed out of use; few contemporary writers said much about them, and we have already seen that notation, regarded purely as a guide to performance, has always been inaccurate and can often be extremely misleading. For medieval music we must be more than ever on our guard against judgements formed by looking at it, as distinct from those based on hearing it performed.

SONORITIES

First of all a very careful attempt must be made to discover the acoustical surroundings in which the music was first performed. The differences between room-music, 'resonant' music and open-air music are at least as marked in the Middle Ages as in the music of later times, and to perform a 'resonant' Mass in a 'dead' studio is as barbarous as to perform a chanson in a concert-hall before an audience of two or three thousand. Inescapably barbarous, perhaps: it is obviously impossible to reproduce a facsimile of a fourteenth- or fifteenth-century performance, but we must do what we can to handle the music properly if we are to understand it at all.

Next, the appropriate instrumental sonorities must be restored. It has been pointed out already that nearly all the instruments have perished, but for the fourteenth and fifteenth centuries sculptures and paintings provide a great deal of fairly reliable evidence, especially for secular music; sacred music is more difficult, for artists tended to become visionary and biblical the moment that angel choirs appeared. Other evidence may be found in the music of the remoter regions of Europe and the Near East. The music and musical instruments heard in the mountains of Sardinia and Sicily, and the bands still used for Catalan dance music are medieval in flavour. The Arabian lute, rebec and shawm are still much the same as they were when they were first introduced into Europe by the Moors.

The singing of Spanish *cante jondo* and *flamenco* singers will give us some idea of how the long vocal roulades found in so much medieval music were probably sung originally; the traditional harp accompaniments to Irish songs noted down by zealous eighteenth-century antiquaries record for us the style of accompaniment favoured, perhaps, at the ducal courts of the fifteenth century.

Broadly speaking it is true to say that the Middle Ages liked their music and musical instruments to be either very loud or very soft. Shawms were as reedy as could be, harpsichords (which used metal plectra) jangled, rebecs snarled, trumpets blared, trumscheits rattled, and organs shook the church to its foundations. Even the quiet instruments were usually louder than their renaissance and baroque descendants: damping mechanisms on dulcimers, harps, psalteries and harpsichords were virtually unknown; lutes were struck with a plectrum of quill or horn, and their tone-colour was enriched by octave strings; harps were strung with wire and plucked with the finger-nails; recorders were larger, fatter and louder than those we see and hear today.

The Middle Ages also had a taste for drones. Bagpipes were drone instruments then as now, of course; but so were medieval fiddles, with their flat bridges and their open drone strings; and portative organs, which had drone pipes any one of which could be made to sound throughout the piece; and double recorders, and hurdy-gurdies. Yet virtually no trace of these drones is ever found in the written music of the time, even though so many instruments possessed them; the player was expected to discover which note of the scale was the tonic, and to adjust his drones accordingly.

Paintings of medieval music-making show that percussion instruments were often used, both large and small; yet once again no trace of them appears in the written musical sources of the time, and a modern editor must do his best to supply appropriate parts for them on the basis of his knowledge of what they can do now and what they might have been asked to do five hundred years ago. Guesswork, indeed: but none the less important and essential to a proper understanding of the music.

Primitive music of our own time, variant readings in the musical sources of the Middle Ages, one or two remarks by theorists, and some special signs used in keyboard music: these provide the evidence for supposing that the medieval musician was as fond of ornamentation in his music as the musician of the renaissance or the baroque periods. Once again the editor has to make guess after guess as to the exact way in which it was used; but it is his responsibility to do so, and he must not shirk it. The sixteenth-century manuals on ornamentation show clearly that they are introducing no new and untried technique; on the contrary their instructions are stylized and systematized in a way that has taken a century or more of continuous thought and development to achieve by the teachers of our own time. In an age before printing was invented, when travel was dangerous, difficult and expensive, and when the pace of life was much slower (though no less erratic, perhaps, than it is now) any comparable development must have taken very much longer; it is safe to assume, therefore, that all the improvisatory techniques in use during the sixteenth century originated at least a century earlier than their first recorded appearance in print, and that many of them may even have been in use in the thirteenth and fourteenth centuries.

The clearest way of outlining some of the problems associated with the performance of medieval music and of suggesting some possible ways in which they may be solved will be to deal with some specific instances—chosen at random, perhaps, and necessarily treated in a very generalized way. These cannot form a solid causeway, but they may at least serve as stepping-stones.

(1) Some fifteenth-century descriptions of music-making. A few detailed accounts of fifteenth-century performances have survived, but very few of them, unfortunately, were written by expert musicians who knew what they were talking about. One reliable authority is Tinctoris, a Flemish theorist and composer who worked at the court of Naples for many years, and was a good musician. Here is a short summary of some remarks from a 'popular' book about music that he wrote in the 1480s; it was published in about 1487.

'In "loud" music, a tenor part is played on a bombard, a

low contratenor[1] (and indeed often any contratenor) on a trombone. Some instruments—the lute, and the vihuela, for instance—can play all four parts of a composition at once, if the player is skilled enough; others—the rebec or the viol—are more restricted. When I was at Bruges some years ago I heard two clever Flemings play many chansons on two viols, the tenor on one and the descant on the other. The gittern is thin in tone and seldom heard in serious music nowadays; the cittern is used by Italian peasants for songs and dances.'

A long account has survived of the extravagant feast given at Lille in 1454 for members of the Order of the Golden Fleece, and it includes some very interesting details of the music performed on this historic occasion. The banqueting hall contained three huge tables, one of which was for the diners. On another there was a model church (complete with stained-glass windows and a bell in the steeple) with three choirboys, a tenor and an organ inside; and the third bore a gigantic pie containing twenty-eight musicians (is this the origin of the nursery rhyme 'Sing a song of sixpence'?). The feast began with a motet from the church. Then a shepherd emerged from the pie, playing a bagpipe, and as soon as he had finished two military trumpeters entered the room on horseback and played a long fanfare. Next, the organ in the church; then a German cornettist from the pie; then a song from the church; then music for lute, dulcian and another instrument from the pie. At the end of the next course four more trumpeters played a loud fanfare; a long organ solo followed from the church, and then a three-part chanson from the pie. Suddenly a twelve-year-old boy came into the hall, riding on a man dressed as a magnificent stag, and the two of them together sang a chanson (by Dufay) called 'I have never seen the like'. The singers in the church then sang a motet, and this was followed by a song for two voices and lute from the pie. Interludes of this kind occurred after each course of the banquet, the music from the pie including a quartet for recorders; two blind beggars with hurdy-gurdies; a lutenist

[1]In the later part of the fifteenth century, contratenors became divided into high contratenors and low contratenors; whence our terms contralto (contratenor altus) and bass (contratenor bassus).

accompanying the singing of a young and beautiful lady-in-waiting; and three players of the pipe-and-tabor.

(2) A fifteenth-century chanson in three parts: 'Puis que je voy, belle' (Arnold de Lantins: HAM 71). The descant of a chanson was usually the first part to be written, and it was often the only part to have words; the other parts were usually instrumental. Chansons were chamber-music, and 'soft' instruments were appropriate for them—the harp, the lute, the pommer, the recorder and the viol. The tenor was composed before the contratenor; it was therefore more important and might be suitably performed on a cantabile melody instrument, the other part being assigned to a lighter tone-colour. The early sixteenth-century Leckingfield proverbs tell us that the shawm is suitable for the lowest part of a piece and the recorder for a middle part; Tinctoris recommended a viol for the tenor and another for the treble. So the sonorities for a chanson à 3 might be:

line 1 (descant):   voice and viol (in bars 13–15, 25–30)
line 2 (tenor):   viol or pommer
line 3 (contratenor): recorder, harp or lute

(3) A fifteenth-century basse-danse: 'La Spagna' (see also HAM 102). The original music for these dances (as opposed to later arrangements) has survived only in the form of tunes in the tenor register, written in long equal notes, and for many years scholars had no idea how this music should be performed. Most pictures of fifteenth-century dancing show the music being provided by a team of three players. In a hall or in the open air, 'loud' instruments were used—shawm, bombard, trombone: in a room, 'soft' ones—recorder, lute and harp, for instance. It has recently been established with a fair degree of certainty that one of the players played straight through the tune as it was written while the others extemporized above it simultaneously; the whole dance would involve four repetitions of the tune, each in a different metre. The whole procedure is astonishingly like that used by the best dance bands of the present day, and it falls into line with what we know about the taste and training of the fifteenth-century musician. Which

instrument played the tenor tune? Probably the bombard or pommer; trombine, psalteries and harps are particularly adapted to playing parts that leap about, and this is a characteristic feature of fifteenth-century contratenors. Possible instrumentations would therefore be:

melodic line	in a room, or for intimate dancing	in a hall, or out of doors
tenor	pommer, tenor viol	bombard
descant (usually improvised)	lute, recorder, treble viol, pipe-and-tabor	shawm
contratenor (usually improvised)	harp, psaltery	trombone

(4) A fifteenth-century sacred work in four parts: Mass *L'Homme armé* (Dufay: HAM 66). This, like most music of the same kind, is written on a tenor *canto fermo* adapted from some other source, sacred or secular (in this case from a secular song), and like all fifteenth-century tenors it must be clearly heard; instruments that suggest themselves as being suitable are the organ (with a full, clear registration of octaves and fifths above the fundamental tone), and bells (sets of these, tuned diatonically but including B ♭ as well as B ♮, were certainly in use in ensemble music, and they had the distinct advantage that they required no tuning once they were made). The other parts were probably sung; or they might have been doubled, or replaced, by cornetts, trombones and slide trumpets. The surroundings were usually highly resonant. Suggestions for performance:

tenor; organ throughout
polyphony *à* 4: chorus and instruments
duos and trios: solo singers (with instrumental interludes, perhaps)

(5) A fifteenth-century carol: 'Alma redemptoris mater' (*Musica Britannica*, vol. IV, no. 4). Carols were processional music, with a recurring burden or refrain, and they were an important feature of fifteenth-century English music. In modern performances the burdens should be sung by a small chorus; these, like much medieval music intended to be performed by a chorus, are often noticeably simpler in style than the more ornate verses on either side of them, which should be sung by soloists. This distinction between music for solo singers and music for chorus can be seen in much fifteenth-century vocal writing, and some manuscripts even use the directions 'duo' and 'chorus' to distinguish between them. But such manuscripts are rare, and the matter was usually left in the hands of the contemporary director of music, who naturally knew all about it. The modern editor ought to help the modern performer by indicating clearly which parts of the music are, in his opinion, to be sung by soloists, and which are to be performed by the whole ensemble; but he seldom does so. As a result old music is often sung by the full choir from beginning to end, which was certainly not the intention of its composers.

In much music of this period, including some carols, the editor must watch for signs that fa-burden was used. One well-known technique of fa-burden could be used to supply a third inner part extempore, when only two parts were written out on the paper; since this technique has been obsolete for centuries, it will be the editor's duty to write the part out in full, to the best of his ability. His version may well be imperfect, but it is better than nothing at all, and far more helpful than a mere footnote.

One possible way of performing this fifteenth-century carol might therefore have been:

burden	chorus *à* 3; the fa-burden line sung by a semi-chorus
verse 1	solo tenor and countertenor voices
burden	chorus *à* 2; fa-burden omitted
verse 2	solo tenor voice; top line played on a lute or viol
burden	semi-chorus singing the tenor; fa-burden (? ornamented) played on a pommer; descant played on two recorders

verse 3	solo countertenor; tenor played on a viol
burden	semi-chorus singing the descant; tenor played on a pommer
verse 4	solo boy singing tenor line transposed up an octave; descant played an octave higher on a viol or psaltery
burden	chorus *à* 2
verse 5	solo tenor voice; top line played on a pommer
burden	chorus *à* 3; all parts doubled at the unison or octave by instruments

It is obviously not easy to find players of the lute, psaltery and pommer, but the guitar, harp and bassoon are good substitutes; and any performance of the varied kind described above will be far more lively and far more authentic than one in which the whole of the music is sung by a full choir from beginning to end.

(6) A fourteenth-century madrigal, or *ballata*. Again there is plenty of evidence to suggest that this was room-music, usually performed by a small ensemble of voices and instruments. The surviving parts are often extremely elaborate, and on the evidence of the instrumental quality of some of the ornamentation certain scholars have concluded that the melodic lines should be split up between voices and instruments. Many fourteenth-century instruments had drones, and these must be re-created by the editors. Many contemporary pictures show that percussion instruments (small sets of bells, triangles, hand-drums) were undoubtedly used, and here again the editor will have to invent parts for them. Variant readings between manuscripts and arrangements of madrigals for keyboard instruments show that the fourteenth-century musician was well acquainted with the techniques of improvised divisions and ornamentation; the editor will probably have to supply divisions and ornaments where he judges them to be necessary. His task, in short, is evidently very great, and his final performing score may well differ very considerably from a strict transcription of the original manuscripts.

Some idea of the size of the problem and of an attempt at its solution will be found on p. 174; here is reproduced (i) a note-for-note transcription of a few bars of Landini's dance-song 'Amor c'al tuo suggetto' (HAM 53) as they appear in the source; and (ii) a score for use today, designed to reproduce something of the probable effect of the music.

(7) A thirteenth-century motet or conductus: a twelfth-century troubadour song. Many of the motets of this period are chamber-music rather than music for use in the services of the church. Some are wholly instrumental, some are for a mixed consort of voices and instruments, and some are entirely for voices. But the student of interpretation finds much to baffle him in the music of this early time, and there is little point in discussing it in any great detail. For one thing, scholars do not wholly agree on the rhythmic interpretation of some of the notational symbols of this period, and the discrepancies between published versions of the same piece taken from the same source are often frighteningly great. On p. 175 the student will find a short section of the top part of a famous three-part conductus 'Hac in anni janua' (HAM 39) as it appears in a thirteenth-century manuscript now in the library at Wolfenbüttel; underneath are two transcriptions of it, each made in accordance with one of the many current theories about the rhythmical interpretation of the notation of this period. On the same page will be found the beginning of a troubadour song by de Ventadorn (d. 1195), as transcribed by three present-day scholars. Clearly any elaborate discussion of sonorities, tempo and phrasing would be rather a waste of time, and performances of this by no means primitive music must for the present remain imperfect and approximate.

(8) Plainsong. In the last chapter it was pointed out that plainsong was probably sung as measured music during much of the Middle Ages and Renaissance. But this was not the only respect in which it differed from the interpretations officially used today. Many early writers encouraged the use of *musica ficta* in plainsong; thus there are some fourteenth-century manuscripts of plainsong in which nearly every cadential F, C or G is sharpened, and a Carthusian Monk writing in 1500 maintained that in plainsong phrases like D F G or G F G the Fs should always be sharpened. To our ears plainsong handled in this way loses one of its special glories, its modality, but there seems little doubt that in

F

plainsong, as in so much other music, early musicians were less modal than we have often wanted to make them. Accidentals, like ornaments, were often a matter of extemporization[1], to be added in accordance with contemporary rules that have long since been forgotten; we may not see them when we look at an early manuscript, but that does not mean that they were equally invisible to a man of the past.

There are some interesting suggestions on plainsong to be found in a little book published in 1474. At major feasts plainsong was to be sung fast, with the quicker notes clearly separated from each other, but on lesser feasts and on most Sundays it was to be sung more slowly. Slight rallentandos at the ends of phrases would help to make the plainsong articulate. Provincialisms like intrusive h's. singing in the nose, and muddling up the vowels were to be avoided; and the singer ought not to add ornaments and cadenzas to the plainsong, as some singers did.

This hint that improvised ornaments and divisions were used even in plainsong can be supported by other evidence dating back to the early years of the twelfth century; but then this is hardly surprising, for the whole of European music has developed out of the techniques of extemporization used by ninth-century monks. Hieronymus of Moravia (*c.* 1260) wrote of the *flos harmonicus*, a plainsong ornament which might be a trill or a mordent according to context and taste; and he gave minute directions dealing with its precise use. Certain plainsong symbols—the *quilisma*, the *trispondens*, the *epiphonus*—are ornaments in themselves, demanding a special technique of singing; but subjects like these belong to a history of notation rather than of performance.

---

[1]For instance, B ♭ and B ♮ seem often to have been regarded by medieval musicians as different aspects of the same note, rather than as different notes. The Solesmes *Antiphonale Monasticum* eliminates many flats, on the grounds that they are not to be found in the earliest manuscripts. It is arguable, however, that singers trained on Guido's system of solmization would have automatically put in the flats, so that there would have been no point in setting them down on the page; and that consequently these 'doubtful' accidentals ought to be retained in a modern edition, not obliterated.

CHAPTER IX

SOME CONCLUSIONS

THERE can be no cut-and-dried set of answers to the questions raised in the performance of early music. The problem itself has only arisen during the last century and a half, for until the early years of the nineteenth century no musician was interested in anything but new music, that is to say, music written during the preceding forty or fifty years. Old manuscripts and printed books were something for the antiquary, the historian and the musical snob; old musical instruments, unless they were violins, were merely old-fashioned and tiresome; and the idea of including even one piece of old music in a concert programme would have been regarded as unfashionable and eccentric.[1]

The reasons for the extraordinary differences between this musical climate and our own would make a fascinating study in themselves, but one that lies well outside the scope of this book. The important thing for us to realize is that a tremendous change has taken place, and that as a result the composer of the present day has to compete for his living with men long dead—many of them unquestioned masters of music in their own time as well as in ours, but others who were once thought of as fine extemporizers and little more. We are imprisoned by the past. The whole upbringing of a modern musician, whether he is a composer, a performer or a listener, is based on playing, hearing, reading and analysing old music. His musical experience has been warped away from the present towards the past; yet the sonorities he hears and the symbols he sees in front of him are those of his own time, so that the past itself is set askew. In an essay written more than thirty years ago, T. S. Eliot remarked that 'the past is altered by the present as much as the present is directed by the past'; and though he was writing of poetry, one does not need to be an Einstein to see

[1]England was to some extent an exception to these generalizations about the performance of 'contemporary' music.

how his remark applies to music. The eighteenth-century musician was taught to see the whole of musical history as a hill rising gently and undulatingly out of darkness, with the music of his own time standing on the sunlit summit; the modern musician is encouraged to view it as a rather alarming slope, studded like Easter Island with titanic heads, far larger than life. And he may even have an uneasy suspicion that the slope is a downward one, and that the noisy and polemical modernists who lead the way are, like the maiden in one of Ernest Bramah's incomparable stories, uttering loud and continuous cries to conceal the direction of their flight.

Upward or downward, the slope is there. The modern musician's approach to the music of his own time is obstructed by the past, and his approach to old music is through the gateway of the present. The figures most familiar to him are the composers of the last two centuries; the sonorities in use are those of the last fifty years, and they are the norm by which he judges the exotic and abnormal tone-colours of marimbas or novachords as well as the exotic and abnormal tone-colours of regals, viols or crumhorns. But to earlier musicians these tone-colours were the normal ones; concert grands, wire-strung violins and Boehm flutes would have been considered strange and abnormal.

All this may seem commonplace enough; but few musicians seem to realize how much it affects their judgements of old music, and that must be the excuse for dealing with it in such detail here. Its relevance to Bach's keyboard music, for instance, is immediate; we cannot answer the simple and direct question: 'Which instrument is the best to use for playing the partita in C minor?', because this question is neither direct nor simple but extremely complex. Each of its component terms bristles with so many difficulties that the question as a whole is almost meaningless. Yet it is asked often enough, and many people seem to be curiously confident they can answer it.

We can begin by discovering which keyboard instruments Bach is known to have played: the harpsichord, the clavichord, the spinet, the organ, the fortepiano and the *Lautenwerck* (a special kind of harpsichord with gut strings, designed to sound like a lute or theorbo). That seems straightforward enough, and most people will have a fairly clear kind of mental image of the tone-colour associated with each word. But this is where the difficulties begin to creep in. One listener's mental image cannot be the same as another's, and neither will be the same as that of a player. None of them can be anything like Bach's; a present-day musician's idea of harpsichord tone-colour is a mixture of the various sounds produced by different players and different instruments, and it is overlaid by a mesh of associations of oldness and strangeness and general quaintness which simply did not exist for Bach. If the harpsichord is an eighteenth-century one, it is old to us; but it was new then, and its sound was not the same. If the harpsichord is a new one, it has all kinds of gadgets and tone-colours (e.g. foot-pedals to change the stops, 16′ strings, and leather plectra), most of which were quite unknown in the eighteenth century. And the same is true for every one of the other instruments in the list.

To discover how these instruments were played in the eighteenth century is even more difficult. There are plenty of tutors, both printed and manuscript, but some are well meaning and unreliable, others represent a highly mannered or very local style, and very few of them are available outside the bigger libraries and museums. Moreover, reading a book will not teach you how to play a musical instrument any more than it will teach you how to paint. Books on piano-playing are dealing with a living tradition; books on harpsichord-playing are corpse-revivers. Meanwhile our unfamiliarity with the harpsichord, with its proper balance with other instruments, and its playing technique turns many present-day 'authentic' performances of old music into mockeries. In unskilled hands the harpsichord, like any other instrument, will usually sound very unpleasant, and conductors and sound engineers can hardly be blamed if they prefer to make Mr X's ugly succession of thuds and twangs as inaudible as possible.

To discover which piece of early music was played by which instrument is more difficult still, as the reader will have discovered for himself long before this. Bach's partitas were almost undoubtedly written for the harpsichord, but it is not usually as easy as this to give an answer. And the older the music the more tricky are the problems of discovering how it was turned into sound.

Here indeed is the cardinal problem. It is possible to discover a great deal about what early music originally sounded like, though the student will need time, patience and judgement. But what should it sound like today? And how should it be played today? The first steps are the responsibility of the editor. He must see to it that the facts found in the original text are set before the players accurately, completely, and intelligibly. 'Nothing shall be imposed . . . without notice of the alteration; nor shall conjecture be wantonly or unnecessarily indulged': Johnson's words, written in large black letters, should hang above the desk of every editor, transcriber, arranger and 'realizer' of old music. Bach's music (or Purcell's or Dufay's) is an inheritance, not a lottery prize. To tarnish it is easy: to squander it, contemptible. To link one's own name to the composer's with a hyphen is to pimp on his capital; to efface his style with one's own is to erase his original inscriptions; to flout the help of the scholar is to debase the composer's coinage; to issue one's own music falsely bearing the name of a man long dead is to mint counterfeit money. All of which sounds very metaphorical and fine, perhaps: yet though we should be justifiably outraged if things like this were allowed to happen to our daily currency, we meekly accept them in the imponderable currency of music, and it is high time that we realized what we are doing.

Assuming for the moment that the editor has been both humble and skilful enough to do his job properly, the next stage is the performer's: the interpretation of the composer's facts as presented by the editor, and their transmutation into sound. His performance must be idiomatic and stylish, no matter what sonorities he uses. Each instrument and each version of the work will display a different facet of the music to the listener, and the player must see that the facets are illuminated brightly and unwaveringly. The performances must be idiomatic; each instrument must be true to itself, and it must not try to ape the others. The harpsichordist must not fuss with the stops in order to try to make his instrument imitate the gradual increase and decrease of tone possible on the piano.

The clavichordist must play delicately and expressively; a clavichord must never sound like a dwarf harpsichord. The pianist must resist the temptation to use octaves in imitation of the harpsichord's 16' and 4' stops, for the effect on his instrument can never be the same. On a harpsichord or an organ the stops are so voiced that they automatically blend into one another, and this blend cannot possibly be produced on an instrument using an entirely different system of tone-production. And the pianist should play Bach, not Bach-Blank, even when Blank happens to be Liszt or Busoni or von Bulow. What these men did was no doubt absolutely right at the time they did it, but to use their versions today is the equivalent of putting on a pair of nineteenth-century spectacles in order to read an eighteenth-century book.

The performances must also be stylish; they must be illuminated by the fullest possible knowledge of the special points of phrasing, ornamentation and tempo that were associated with the music when it was first heard. The performer has every right to decide for himself that some of these special points are best forgotten; but he must at least be aware that they once existed, and that they were at some time considered to be an essential feature of a pleasing performance. Otherwise he risks throwing out the good with the bad, and the baby with the bathwater.

Little has been said so far about the listener, yet he has a contribution to make to the music as well. Listening to music is not something passive and inert; it is an active occupation. The composer, the editor and the performer are setting out to meet the listener at his own invitation; and a host has more to do than just sitting and waiting for his guests to arrive. Rooms must be made ready for them, and the courteous host will go part of the way to meet them. Metaphors and analogies again: but they are the most forceful way of putting the point. The listener must not expect to understand any music unless he knows what its composer was trying to say and how he set about saying it, and this is as true of Bach, Byrd and Binchois as it is of Alban Berg.

It is impossible for anyone living today to hear early music with the ears of those who first heard it, and it is idle to pretend otherwise. But it is more or less possible for us to look at its notation with the eyes of those who first saw it, and the least we can do is to try. Too few editors realize their responsibilities not only to the composer but also to the present-day performer. Too few performers realize the nature of the contribution they must make to the performance; in interpretation style is at least as important as size, and both are needed. No music, least of all old music, must be played listlessly and boringly, for music has always been written to be enjoyed both by the player and the listener; yet all music must sound spontaneous, and the performer must not worry at it like a dog with a bone. Old music is not necessarily slow music. It is easy to fall into this trap if we read musical notation without an adequate understanding of how it has changed and developed during the course of the centuries; but if the edition is a good one, the performer can safely trust his eyes, his musicianship and his common sense. Old music needs time to breathe; it is neither a race nor a waterslide. Above all, the written text must never be regarded as a dead laboratory specimen; it is only sleeping, though both love and time will be needed to awaken it. But love and time will be wasted without a sense of tradition and of historical continuity, and these are not to be inherited nor are they easily acquired. Music is both an art and a science; like every art and every science it has no enemy save ignorance.

MUSICAL ILLUSTRATIONS

The opening bars of the Overture to Lully's opera *Alceste* (HAM 224) as they would have been performed by an orchestra trained to play in the French style. See p. 85.

An Adagio graced in the Italian *galant* style, from Quantz's book on flute-playing (1752). The expression marks, like the ornaments, are by Quantz himself. See p. 97.

F*

Six suggestions for ornamenting one bar of an Adagio by Tartini,
taken from Cartier's violin school of 1798; these show how the tradition of improvised ornamentation of slow movements continued into
the nineteenth century. See p. 88.

The opening of a Largo from Purcell's Trio-sonata in E minor, as it appears in the original edition and as it should be played. See p. 126.

A violin melody bowed in the French and Italian styles by Georg Muffat, showing the contrast between them. See p. 94.

Some variant readings listed in the ten volumes of *Tudor Church Music*. They look like written-out divisions on the basic vocal text, suggesting that this distinctively Italian sixteenth-century technique was also known in England. See p. 147.

The beginning and ending of Cipriano di Rore's madrigal 'A la dolc'
ombra' with divisions by Girolamo dalla Casa (1584); the divisions are
given in smaller notes. See p. 143.

The opening bars of a ballata by Francesco Landini (*d.* 1397), first in a strict transcription, and then in a version designed to produce something of the effect of a fourteenth-century performance. See p. 160.

Part of the thirteenth-century conductus *Hac in anni janua* first as it appears in the manuscripts and then in two (conflicting) transcriptions. See p. 161.

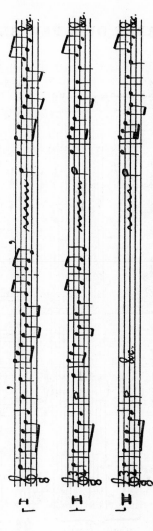

Parts of an unaccompanied song *Be m'an perdut* by the troubadour Bernart de Ventadorn (who died in 1195) as transcribed by three different modern scholars. See p. 161.

TABLE OF A FEW SELECTED ORNAMENTS

GLOSSARY

A cappella: Unaccompanied choral singing.

acciaccatura: a grace-note, played as short as possible (see table).

appoggiatura (port de voix): A single ornamental note, slow, on the beat (see table).

Baroque: 1575–1750.

bassanelli: Renaissance wind instruments. No details known.

bombard: Medieval reed instrument, loud.

Chitarrone: Arch-lute, 6′ tall, strung with wire strings, used for continuo-playing.

cittern: Small plucked instrument, wire-strung, for informal music.

clavichord: Wire-strung keyboard instrument, strings pressed by 'tangents' of brass. Tone gentle and very expressive.

conductus: a form of medieval vocal music in which the parts moved in note-against-note counterpoint to the same words.

contemporary: Used throughout this book with the meaning it has in the sentence 'Bach was contemporary with Handel'.

continuo: A mainly chordal accompaniment improvised from a figured or unfigured bass.

cornett: Early wind instrument of wood, cup mouth-piece, finger holes. **Mute cornett:** Specially soft cornett, for chamber music.

coulé: Ornamental note, played before the beat, usually filling the gaps in a chain of descending thirds (see table).

crumhorn: Early reed instrument, shaped like a fishhook, reed enclosed in a capsule, out of reach of the player's lips.

Division: Improvised variation on a theme.

dulcian: Renaissance reed instrument, bassoon-like, very soft.

dulcimer: Wire-strung instrument struck with wire hammers, one in each hand.

Fa-burden: Improvised harmonization of a theme, mainly in 6/3 chords, English in origin, current in fifteenth and sixteenth centuries.

falso-bordone: Homophonic harmonizations of short plain-songs (psalm-tones, Magnificats), used in renaissance Italy and Spain.

fortepiano: Later eighteenth-century grand or square piano.

Galant: A musical style current from *c.* 1725 to *c.* 1775.

gittern: Ancestor of guitar, gut-strung.

Harpsichord (clavecin, cembalo): Wire-strung keyboard instrument, strings plucked by jacks bearing plectra of quill or (later) leather. May have more than one manual and several different tone-colours.

hurdy-gurdy (organistrum): Medieval gut-strung instrument with drone strings, sounded by a rosin-covered wheel, melody strings stopped by tangents controlled from a primitive keyboard.

Lira (lirone): Renaissance string instrument, bowed, gut-strung, often with drone strings. The bass lira (*lirone*) was for continuo-playing.

Long: a medieval note-value worth two or three breves.

lyra bastarda: Small bass-viol for brilliant divisions and passage-work.

Medieval: Pre-1500.

messa di voce: Vocal ornament; a sustained note swelled and then diminished (see table).

mordent (pincé, quiebro): Ornament (see table).

Natural trumpet (horn): Valveless, capable of sounding only the natural harmonics (before 1750).

Pipe-and-tabor: Dance instrument; pipe played by one hand, tabor (drum) struck by the other.

pommer: Medieval reed instrument, soft.

portative (organetto): Very small organ (one rank of pipes, maximum range two octaves), blown with left hand and played by the right. A melody instrument.

psaltery: Medieval dulcimer, strings plucked by fingers or finger-nails.

Ranket: Renaissance reed instrument, bassoon-like, in the shape of a cylinder no more than 6″ high and 4″ in diameter. Very muffled tone.

rebec: Medieval string instrument, small, bowed, gut-strung, belly of skin. Snarling, reedy tone.

recorder: End-blown, eight-holed whistle flute.

regal: Renaissance reed keyboard instrument, not unlike harmonium but smaller and more noble in tone; beating reeds of brass.

renaissance: 1480–1625.

Schryari: Shrill reed instrument of Renaissance. No details known.

shawm: Commonest medieval reed instrument.

slide: Ornament (see table).

spinet: Wire-strung keyboard instrument, wing-shaped, strings plucked by quilled jacks, one tone-colour, one manual.

Tablatures: Special notational systems used for certain harmony instruments (lute, organ, etc.) and occasionally for melody instruments.

theorbo: Large lute with two necks, one carrying open strings; gut-strung.

triangle: The jangle of the medieval triangle was increased by wire rings hung on the cross-bar.

trill (tremblement): Ornament (see table).

trumscheit: Medieval one-stringed instrument, bowed, sounding only the natural harmonics. The bass trumscheit was revived in the seventeenth century as the *tromba marina*.

Use: the special liturgy and order of service associated with a particular diocese.

Vihuela: Spanish lute, sixteenth century.

viol family (division viol, violone): Stringed instruments, bowed underhand, six gut strings, fretted neck, flat back. All sizes held on or between legs; hence the Italian family name *viola da gamba*. **Division viol:** small bass viol for division-playing. **Violone:** double-bass viol.

violin family: Stringed instruments, bowed overhand, four gut strings, arched back. All sizes except the largest held over left arm and against breast (later, under chin); hence the Italian family name *viola da braccio*.

virginals: Renaissance and early baroque wire-strung keyboard instrument, rectangular, quilled jacks mounted in a diagonal row across the soundboard.

LIST OF SOURCES

A. AGAZZARI (1607): *Del sonare sopra'l Basso.* Facsimile: Milan, 1933. English translation in Arnold (1931), Strunk (1951).
M. AGRICOLA (1528–9): *Musica instrumentalis deudsch.*
N. AMMERBACH (1571): *Orgel oder Instrument Tabulatur.*
F. T. ARNOLD (1931): *The Art of Accompaniment from a Thorough-bass.*
C. AVISON (1752): *An Essay on Musical Expression.*
—— (1756): Preface to *Six Sonatas for the Harpsichord . . . Opera Quinta.*
C. P. E. BACH (1753): *Versuch über die wahre Art das Clavier zu Spielen.* Reprint: Leipzig, 1925 (5th ed.). English translation: *Essay on the true art of playing keyboard instruments*: New York and London, 1949.
DOM BÉDOS DE CELLES (1766): *L'art du facteur d'orgues.* Facsimile: Cassel, 1934–6.
J. BERMUDO (1549, 1555): *Declaraciõ de Instrumentos.*
F. BIANCIARDI (1607): *Breve regola per imparar sonare sopra il Basso.* English translation in Arnold (1931).
J. BLOW (MS): B.M. Add. MS 34072. Printed: Arnold (1931).
E. BOTTRIGARI (1594): *Il Desiderio.* Facsimile: Berlin, 1924.
S. BROSSARD (1703): *Dictionnaire de Musique.*
P. BRUNOLD: *Traité des signes et agréments employés par les clavecinistes français . . .* (1935).
C. BUTLER (1636): *Principles of Musik.*

P. CERONE (1613): *El Melopeo.* English extracts: Strunk (1951).
A. PETIT COCLICO (1552): *Compendium musices.* Facsimile: Cassel, 1955.
M. R. COELHO (1620): *Flores de Musica.*
F. COUPERIN (1716): Preface to *Second livre de pièces de clavecin.*
—— (1716–17): *L'art de toucher le clavecin.* Reprinted: Paris, 1933 (complete works); Leipzig, 1933 (with English translation).
J. S. COUSSER (1682): *Composition de musique Suivant la Méthode française.*
G. DALLA CASA (1584): *Il vero modo di diminuir, Lib.* 1 & 2.

E. DANNREUTHER: *Musical Ornamentation* (1893).
C. DE ARRAUXO (1626): *Facultad Organica.* Reprint: Barcelona, 1948–52.
DE FRENEUSE (1704–5): *Comparaison de la musique italienne et de la musique françoise.* English extracts in Strunk (1951).
DE MAROLLES (1657): *Mémoires.*
DE ST. LAMBERT (1702): *Les principes du clavecin.*
T. DE SANTA MARIA (1565): *Arte de tañer Fantasia . . .*
G. DIRUTA (1593?, 1597): *Il Transilvano.*
A. DOLMETSCH: *The Interpretation of the Music of the XVIIth and XVIIIth centuries* (1915).

H. FINCK (1556): *Practica Musica.*

J. E. GALLIARD (1724): translation of Tosi's *Art of Florid Song.*
S. GANASSI (1542–3): *Regola Rubertina.* Facsimile: Leipzig, 1924.
F. GEMINIANI (1751): *The Art of Playing on the Violin.* Facsimile: London, 1952.
—— (c. 1745): *Rules for Playing in a true Taste.*

H. GERLE (1532–3): *Musica teutsch.*

DR. GREGORY (1766): *A Comparative view of the State and Faculties of Man* . . . (3rd edition).

R. E. M. HARDING (1938): *Origins of Musical Time and Expression.*

E. HOLMES (1828): *A Ramble among the Musicians of Germany.*

J. HOTTETERRE (1728): *Principes de la Flute traversiere.* Facsimile: Cassel 1941.

W. JACKSON (1791): *Observations on the present State of Music in London.*

H. JUDENKÜNIG (1523): *Ain schone kunstliche underweisung.*

A. KIRCHER (1650): *Musurgia universalis.*

M. L'AFFILARD (1694): *Principes très-faciles pour bien apprendre la musique.*

M. LOCKE (1656): Preface to *Little Consort of Three Parts.*

—— (1673): *Melothesia.* Section on continuo-playing reprinted in Arnold (1931).

E. LOULIÉ (1696): *Elements ou principes de la Musique.*

T. MACE (1676): *Musick's Monument.* Facsimile: Paris, 1959.

M. MARAIS (1692): Preface to *Pièces en Trio.*

F. W. MARPURG (1755): *Anleitung zum Clavierspielen.*

—— (1758): *Anleitung zur Singcomposition.*

V. MARTINELLI (1768): *Lettere famigliari e critiche.*

J. MATTHESON (1739): *Der volkommene Capellmeister.* Facsimile: Cassel, 1956.

M. MERSENNE (1636): *Harmonie Universelle.*

C. MERULO (1592): *Canzoni d'Intavolatura d'Organo.* Reprint: Cassel, 1941.

J. J. C. DE MONDONVILLE (1734): *Pièces de clavecin en sonates.* Reprint: Paris, 1935.

T. MORLEY (1597): *A Plaine and Easie Introduction to Practicall Musicke.* Facsimile: London, 1937. Reprint: London and New York, 1952.

L. MOZART (1756): *Versuch einer gründlichen Violinschule.* Reprint: London, 1948.

G. MUFFAT (1695): *Florilegium I.* Reprint: *Denkmäler der Tonkunst in Österreich,* I.

—— (1698): *Florilegium II.* Reprint: ibid., II.

—— (1701): *Auserlesene . . . Instrumental-Music.* Reprint: ibid., XI. Extracts in English from all three prefaces in Strunk (1951).

A. NOTARI (1613): *Prime Musiche Nuove.*

D. ORTIZ (1553): *Trattado de Glosas.* Reprints: Berlin, 1913, and Cassel, 1936.

J. PLAYFORD (1654): *Introduction to the Skill of Musick.*

M. PRAETORIUS (1615–19): *Syntagma Musicum,* Facsimile (of the *Organographia*): Cassel, 1929. Incomplete reprints: Leipzig, 1884, 1894, 1916.

H. PURCELL (1696): Preface to *A choice Collection of Lessons.* Reprint: London, 1895 (Purcell Society).

J. J. QUANTZ (1752): *Versuch einer Anweisung die Flöte traversiere zu spielen.* Reprint: Leipzig, 1906. Facsimile: Cassel, 1953. English extracts in Strunk (1951).

F. RAGUENET (1702): *Parallèle des Italiens et des François.* English extracts in Strunk (1951).

T. ROBINSON (1603): *The Schoole of Musicke.*

J. ROUSSEAU (1687): *Traité de la viole.*

A. Schlick (1511): *Spiegel der Orgelmacher*. Reprints: Leipzig, 1869; Mainz, 1932, 1937.

C. Simpson (1667): *The Division-Viol*. Facsimile: London, 1955.

O. Strunk (1951): *Source Readings in Music History*. English edition: London, 1952.

O. Tigrini (1588): *Compendio della Musica*.

J. Tinctoris (c. 1487): *De usu et inventione musicae*. Reprint: Regensburg, 1917. English translation (incomplete): *Galpin Society Journal*, III.

T. Tomkins (1668): *Musica Deo Sacra, Pars Organica*.

J. Van Der Elst (1657): *Notae Augustianae* . . .

N. Vicentino (1555): *L'Antica Musica*. . . .

S. Virdung (1511): *Musica getutscht*. Facsimile: Cassel, 1931.

W. Young (1653): *Sonate a 3, 4, 5 voci*. Incomplete edition: London, 1930.

G. Zarlino (1558): *Le Istitutioni harmoniche*. English extracts in Strunk (1951).

SUGGESTIONS FOR FURTHER READING

A BAINES: *Woodwind Instruments and their History* (London, 1957).

A. CARSE: *The Orchestra in the Eighteenth Century* (Cambridge, 1940).

R. DONINGTON: 'On Interpreting Early Music', *Music & Letters*, XXVIII.

T. S. ELIOT: 'Tradition and the Individual Talent' (in Selected Essays).

W. EMERY: *Bach's Ornaments* (London, 1953).

E. FERAND: *Die Improvisation in Beispielen* (Cologne, 1956).

E. FERAND: *Die Improvisation in der Musik* (Zurich, 1938).

The Galpin Society Journal (London, 1948 to date).

F. GHISI: *Feste Musicali della Firenze Medicea* (Florence, 1939).

H. GOLDSCHMIDT: *Die Lehre von der vokalen Ornamentik* (Charlottenburg, 1907).

Grove's Dictionary of Music and Musicians (5th edition), in particular the articles on 'Baroque Interpretation', 'Expression', 'Fingering: Keyboard', 'Harpsichord Playing', 'Notation', 'Ornamentation', 'Ornaments', and on individual musical instruments.

R. HAAS: *Aufführungspraxis der Musik* (Potsdam, 1931).

E. HARICH-SCHNEIDER: *The Harpsichord* (Cassel, 1954).

R. KIRKPATRICK: *Domenico Scarlatti* (Princeton, 1953).

M. KUHN: *Die Verzierungskunst in der Gesangsmusik . . .* (Leipzig, 1902).

C. SACHS: *The Commonwealth of Art* (New York, 1946).

C. SACHS: *Rhythm and Tempo* (New York and London, 1953).

A. SCHERING: *Aufführungspraxis alter Musik* (Leipzig, 1931).

A. SCHERING: 'Zur instrumentale Verzierungskunst im 18ten Jahrhundert', *Sammelbände der I.M.G.*, VII.

H. P. SCHMITZ: *Die Kunst der Verzierung im 18. Jahrhundert* (Cassel, 1955).

H. P. SCHMITZ: *Prinzipien der Aufführungspraxis alter Musik* (Berlin, 1950).

INDEX

This index is selective. For "allemande", "galliard", etc., see Dance-forms
For "Allegro", "Largo", etc., see Tempo. Reference should also be made to
the Glossary and to the List of Sources.